Contents

Grade 4 Standards—Reading: Informational Text

A. Key Ideas and Details	
	1. Refer to details and examples in a text when explaining what the text says explicitly and when drawing inferences from the text.
	2. Determine the main idea of a text and explain how it is supported by key details; summarize the text.
	3. Explain events, procedures, ideas, or concepts in a historical, scientific, or technical text, including what happened and why, based on specific information in the text.
B. Craft and Structure	
	1. Determine the meaning of general academic and domain-specific words or phrases in a text relevant to a *grade 4 topic or subject area.*
	2. Describe the overall structure (e.g., chronology, comparison, cause/effect, problem/solution) of events, ideas, concepts, or information in a text or part of a text.
	3. Compare and contrast a firsthand and secondhand account of the same event or topic; describe the differences in focus and the information provided.
C. Integration of Knowledge and Ideas	
	1. Interpret information presented visually, orally, or quantitatively (e.g., in charts, graphs, diagrams, time lines, animations, or interactive elements on Web pages) and explain how the information contributes to an understanding of the text in which it appears.
	2. Explain how an author uses reasons and evidence to support particular points in a text.
	3. Integrate information from two texts on the same topic in order to write or speak about the subject knowledgeably.
D. Range of Reading and Level of Text Complexity	
	1. By the end of year, read and comprehend informational texts, including history/social studies, science, and technical texts, in the grades 4–5 text complexity band proficiently, with scaffolding as needed at the high end of the range.

Visit www.creativeteaching.com to find out how this book correlates to Common Core and/or State Standards.

Reading Passages Specific Standards

Text	A. 1	A. 2	A. 3	B. 1	B. 2	B.3	C. 1	C. 2	C. 3	D. 1
Who Invented That? (p. 6)	✔	✔	✔	✔					N/A	✔
Making Silk in Ancient China (p. 8)	✔	✔			✔				N/A	✔
Rivers of Life (p. 10)		✔			✔				N/A	✔
Egypt's Women Pharaohs (p. 12)	✔		✔	✔	✔				N/A	✔
Slavery in Ancient Rome (p. 15)			✔	✔		✔			N/A	✔
Games Across the Ages (p. 18)	✔	✔		✔					N/A	✔
The History of Bicycles (p. 20)	✔	✔	✔		✔				N/A	✔
Our Growing Cities (p. 22)	✔		✔	✔	✔				N/A	✔
Eating Breakfast (p. 25)	✔	✔	✔	✔					N/A	✔
Why Playing Sports Is Good for You (p. 27)	✔	✔			✔			✔	N/A	✔
Turn Down the Music! (p. 29)	✔		✔		✔		✔		N/A	✔
When You See Bullying (p. 31)	✔			✔	✔			✔	N/A	✔
Be a Good Sport! (p. 33)	✔			✔				✔	N/A	✔
Fact Sheet: Peer Pressure (p. 36)	✔				✔				N/A	✔
The Truth About *Tyrannosaurus Rex* (p. 39)	✔	✔		✔				✔	N/A	✔
Where Did the Lions Go? (p. 42)	✔	✔		✔			✔		N/A	✔
Growing Up (p. 44)	✔				✔		✔		N/A	✔
Habitat Communities (p. 47)	✔	✔	✔		✔				N/A	
How Does That Help? (p. 49)	✔		✔	✔	✔				N/A	✔
Producers, Consumers, and Decomposers (p. 52)	✔		✔		✔		✔		N/A	✔
Deforestation (p. 54)	✔		✔					✔	N/A	✔
A Sound Experiment (p. 56)	✔	✔	✔	✔					N/A	✔
How Hard Is That? (p. 59)	✔						✔	✔	N/A	✔
Magnets Are More Than Fun (p. 62)	✔		✔	✔					N/A	✔
A Star Is Born (p. 64)	✔		✔	✔	✔				N/A	✔
Seeing Stars (p. 67)	✔		✔	✔			✔		N/A	✔
The World at Night (p. 69)	✔	✔	✔	✔			✔		N/A	✔
Earthquake! (p. 71)	✔		✔		✔	✔	✔		N/A	✔
What Does a Marine Biologist Do? (p. 75)	✔		✔	✔			✔		N/A	✔
What Does a Carpenter Do? (p. 77)	✔			✔			✔		N/A	✔
What Does a Firefighter Do? (p. 79)	✔	✔		✔				✔	N/A	✔
Roald Dahl (p. 81)	✔	✔		✔				✔	N/A	✔
Spider-Man (p. 84)	✔			✔	✔			✔	N/A	✔
Who Was Paul Bunyan? (p. 86)	✔	✔		✔				✔	N/A	✔
Marie Curie (p. 88)	✔		✔						N/A	✔
Annie Oakley (p. 91)	✔		✔	✔					N/A	✔
The Goose and the Golden Eggs (p. 94)	✔			✔					N/A	✔
The Rich Miser (p. 96)	✔		✔	✔					N/A	✔
The Rich Man and the Thief (p. 98)	✔		✔	✔					N/A	✔

Introduction

Reading comprehension is the cornerstone of a child's academic success. By completing the activities in this book, children will develop and reinforce essential reading comprehension skills. Children will benefit from a wide variety of opportunities to practice engaging with text as active readers who can self-monitor their understanding of what they have read.

Children will focus on the following:

Identifying the Purpose of the Text
- The reader understands, and can tell you, why they read the text.

Understanding the Text
- What is the main idea of the text?
- What are the supporting details?
- Which parts are facts and which parts are opinions?

Analyzing the Text
- How does the reader's background knowledge enhance the text clues to help the reader answer questions about the text or draw conclusions?
- What inferences can be made by using information from the text with what the reader already knows?
- How does the information from the text help the reader make predictions?
- What is the cause and effect between events?

Making Connections
How does the topic or information they are reading remind the reader about what they already know?
- Text-to-self connections: How does this text relate to your own life?
- Text-to-text connections: Have I read something like this before? How is this text similar to something I have read before? How is this text different from something I have read before?
- Text-to-world connections: What does this text remind you of in the real world?

Using Text Features
- How do different text features help the reader?

Text Features

Text features help the reader to understand the text better. Here is a list of text features with a brief explanation on how they help the reader.

Contents	Here the reader will find the title of each section, what page each text starts on within sections, and where to find specific information.
Chapter Title	The chapter title gives the reader an idea of what the text will be about. The chapter title is often followed by subheadings within the text.
Title and Subheading	The title or topic is found at the top of the page. The subheading is right above a paragraph. There may be more than one subheading in a text.
Map	Maps help the reader understand where something is happening. It is a visual representation of a location.
Diagram and Illustration	Diagrams and illustrations give the reader additional visual information about the text.
Label	A label tells the reader the title of a map, diagram, or illustration. Labels also draw attention to specific elements within a visual.
Caption	Captions are words that are placed underneath the visuals. Captions give the reader more information about the map, diagram, or illustration.
Fact Box	A fact box tells the reader extra information about the topic.
Table	A table presents text information in columns and rows in a concise and often comparative way.
Bold and Italic text	**Bold** and *italic* text are used to emphasize a word or words, and signify that this is important vocabulary.

Who Invented That?

Mesopotamia is called the "**cradle of civilization**" because it was the first place where people came together to live in one place. First there were small villages and towns. Some towns became large cities as the population grew. **Governments** were formed to take care of the people.

There were many things that helped Mesopotamia grow. Many of these inventions are as important today as they were then.

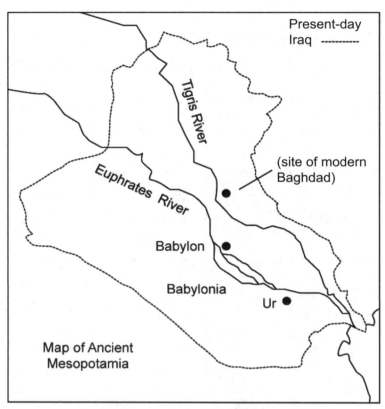

Mesopotamia was in present-day Iraq between two rivers—the Tigris and the Euphrates.

The Wheel

Scientists do not know for sure who invented the first wheel. Many say the people of Mesopotamia did. Many agree that Mesopotamians were the first people to use the wheel for everyday things. They used a potter's wheel to make pots. They used carts with wheels to move goods from place to place. Carts helped towns and cities **trade** with other places. Trade meant they could sell things they did not need and buy from other people things they needed.

Irrigation

Farmers in Mesopotamia needed lots of water from the rivers to grow crops. Carrying water by hand or in carts was hard work. It took a lot of time. Mesopotamians invented **irrigation** so they could have bigger farms and would not have to work so hard. They dug **canals** that would bring water from the rivers to their farms.

The Seeder Plow

Farmers needed to plow the fields before they could plant seeds. Then they had to go back to put seeds in the ground. The Mesopotamians invented the **seeder plow**. In the seeder plow, there was a funnel with seeds behind the plow. As the plow dug up the soil, the seeds were dropped into the soil right away. This meant that farmers could plant more crops in a shorter time.

People from Mesopotamia also invented the first writing system, the first sailboat, and the first 12-month calendar. They were a remarkable civilization.

"Who Invented That?"—Think About It

1. Why is Mesopotamia called the "cradle of civilization"?

_____

_____

_____

2. How did trade help the people of Mesopotamia?

_____

_____

_____

3. What do you think the word _remarkable_ means? Use details from the text to support your answer.

_____

_____

_____

4. What happened when the Mesopotamians invented irrigation?

_____

_____

_____

5. What problem did the invention of the seeder plow solve?

_____

_____

_____

6. What is the purpose of this text? Why do you think the author wrote it?

_____

_____

_____

Making Silk in Ancient China

The making of **silk fabric** was one of the most important discoveries in ancient China. The ancient Chinese discovered that **silkworms** make tiny strands of **silk**, and these strands can be used to make a **fabric** that is beautiful and very strong. Read on to find out how the ancient Chinese made silk.

Step 1: The eggs laid by silkworm moths are collected and kept in a cool place where the **temperature** can be controlled. Over time, the temperature is slowly increased to about 77°F (25°C). The silkworms will then **hatch** from the eggs.

Step 2: Silkworms are fed fresh **mulberry leaves**. They eat constantly until they grow very fat. The fat provides the **energy** the silkworms need to create a **cocoon**.

Step 3: Silkworms produce a **jelly-like material** that hardens into a thin **strand** of silk when it is exposed to air. The worm wraps itself in the long strand to create a white cocoon.

Step 4: The cocoons are kept in a dry place for several days. The cocoons are then **steamed** or **baked** to kill the silkworm inside before it starts to break out. Each cocoon is then dipped in hot water to loosen the strand of silk.

Step 5: Each cocoon is then unwound to get the long strand of silk. This strand is between 656 yards (600 meters) and 984 yd (900 m) long. The strands are then wound onto a **spool**.

Step 6: Several strands of silk are then **twisted together** to make strong silk **thread**. Natural materials are used to **dye** the threads different colors. The threads are then woven into colorful fabric.

Silkmoth

Silkworm

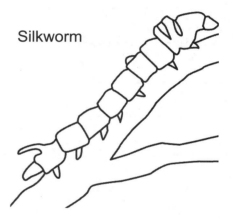

Silk cocoon

Fun Fact

According to Chinese legend, Empress Hsi Ling Shi, wife of Emperor Huang Ti (also called the Yellow Emperor), was the first person to accidentally discover silk. It happened when a silkworm cocoon fell into the cup of tea she was drinking under a mulberry tree. When she pulled out the cocoon, the strong silk fiber came loose.

"Making Silk in Ancient China"—Think About It

1. Complete the chart to show causes and effects in the text.

Cause	Effect
The temperature where the eggs are kept reaches about 77°F (25°C).	
	The silkworms have enough energy to create a cocoon.
	The jelly-like material hardens into a thin strand of silk.
The cocoons are steamed or baked.	
	The strand of silk that makes up the cocoon becomes loose.
	Strong silk thread is created.

2. What is the main idea of the text?

_____

_____

3. How do you know that it takes a lot of energy for a silkworm to create a cocoon?

_____

_____

Rivers of Life

Thousands and thousands of years ago, humans lived in small groups. They traveled to find food and shelter. Then they started to live in larger and larger groups. They began living in one place and growing some of their own food. Most of the places where these people settled were near or on rivers. Why?

The Nile River

The Nile River flows through five countries in Africa. One of these countries is Egypt.

One of the oldest civilizations in the world began in Egypt. Most of Egypt was desert, but the Nile River created a green

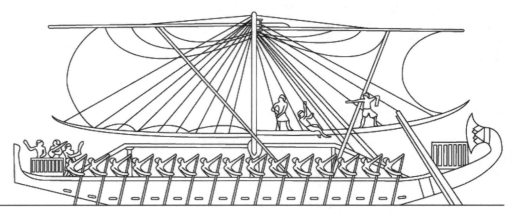

Queen Hatshepsut's sailing boat traveled the Nile.

space along its banks. The land around the river was very flat. The river flooded every year from water that came rushing down from mountains in another country. After the flood, people planted their crops in the thick mud left behind. The mud was very good for growing crops. These crops provided food for the people and their animals. People fished in the river and caught birds for food. The river also provided transportation. People could use boats to travel from town to town to trade.

The Indus River

The Indus River starts in the Himalayan Mountains. It flows through what is now Pakistan. The Indus River is in a very dry area. One of the earliest civilizations in the world began here, just like in Egypt. The river flooded at least once a year. It brought good soil along with it, and left the soil behind. This soil was excellent for farming. The flooding also provided water for irrigation. Farmers grew crops such as melons, wheat, peas, and cotton. Historians believe that there were more than 1,500 settlements in the valley created by the Indus River.

The River Thames

Great cities also began on rivers. London, England, is one example. London is on the River Thames. The city was first built by the Romans. It was called Londinium. After the Romans left, people continued to live in and move to London. The river provided people with transportation. Ships could come in from the sea, and goods could be moved into England. So London became an inland port and a major trading city. Many crafts people lived and worked in London because it was easy to ship what they made to the rest of England and other parts of the world.

"Rivers of Life"—Think About It

1. How is this text organized? What is the author comparing?

_____

_____

_____

2. What is the same about the land around the Nile and Indus Rivers?

_____

_____

_____

3. How did the flooding of the Nile and Indus Rivers help farmers?

_____

_____

_____

4. What was the most important use of the River Thames?

_____

_____

_____

5. What are the sections on the Nile River and the Indus River about? What is the main idea of both?

_____

_____

_____

6. What is the section on the River Thames about? How is this different from the other two sections?

_____

_____

_____

Egypt's Women Pharaohs

The ancient Egyptian civilization lasted for 3,000 years. Egypt was ruled by **pharaohs** during most of that time. Pharaohs were like kings or emperors. Some Egyptians believed that pharaohs were gods.

Pharaohs came from one family or **dynasty**. Thirty families ruled ancient Egypt at different times. It was usually a war that ended a dynasty or family line. Then another family would take over and become pharaohs.

The eldest son of the pharaoh would become the next pharaoh after his father died. If there were no sons, another male relative would become pharaoh. Sometimes women became pharaohs, but this did not happen often. Two of the best known women pharaohs were Hatshepsut and Cleopatra.

Hatshepsut

Hatshepsut (*Hat-shep-soot*) was a royal princess. When Hatshepsut's husband Thutmose II died, his son Thutmose III was too young to be pharaoh. His **stepmother** Hatshepsut ruled Egypt for him as pharaoh for 22 years. It was hard to be a woman pharaoh. She had to be very smart to keep power. Instead of fighting with other countries, she traded with them. This made Egypt a very rich country. She built many important buildings throughout Egypt. She started dressing like a male pharaoh. She even wore a fake beard. She said that she was the daughter of a **god**.

Hatshepsut

After she died, her stepson Thutmose III became pharaoh. He **destroyed** her statues and anything that had her name on it. This was probably because she took the rule of Egypt away from him when he was very young.

Cleopatra

Cleopatra was also a royal princess. Her family had **ruled** Egypt for 300 years. When Cleopatra's father died, he gave the **throne** to her and her younger brother. Her brother forced her from the throne. Cleopatra made a **partnership** with Julius Caesar, one of the leaders of Rome. His army **defeated** her brother and Cleopatra became pharaoh on her own.

Cleopatra was very smart. She spoke seven languages. She also claimed to be an Egyptian god in human form. Cleopatra built up Egypt's trade with other countries. During her rule, Egypt was very **wealthy**, and she was very popular.

Cleopatra

In the end though, she was defeated in war by another Roman leader. Then Rome began to rule Egypt. Cleopatra was the last pharaoh of Egypt.

"Egypt's Women Pharaohs"—Think About It

1. What is another name for the families that ruled Egypt as pharaohs?

_____

_____

2. What happened after Cleopatra made a partnership with Julius Caesar?

_____

_____

_____

_____

_____

3. Why was it unusual for a woman to become a pharaoh?

_____

_____

_____

_____

_____

4. Why do you think Hatshepsut dressed like a male pharaoh?

_____

_____

_____

_____

_____

5. How were Hatshepsut and Cleopatra the same?

_____

_____

_____

6. Did the Romans rule Egypt as pharaohs? How do you know?

_____

_____

_____

_____

7. What is the same and different about the ways Hatshepsut and Cleopatra came to be pharaoh?

_____

_____

_____

_____

8. Why do you think Hatshepsut and Cleopatra built up trade with other countries?

_____

_____

_____

9. Hatshepsut claimed to be the daughter of a god and Cleopatra said she was a god in human form. Why do you think they made those claims?

_____

_____

_____

_____

Slavery in Ancient Rome

A Life of Slavery

Slaves were very important in Ancient Rome. They did most of the work that people would get paid for today.

Who were these slaves? Some were soldiers captured in battle and sent back to Rome as slaves. Some were children who had no parents.

There were two groups of slaves: **public** and **private**. Public slaves were owned by the government. They took care of public buildings. They built roads and cleaned sewers. Some worked as clerks and tax collectors for the city.

Private slaves were owned by **individuals**. Not all slaves did the same kinds of jobs. Some, such as Greeks, were well educated. They might work as teachers or doctors. Others were domestic slaves. They worked as cooks, maids, hairdressers, and tailors in households. Others worked on farms or in mines. Some became gladiators.

Nearly everyone who was a Roman citizen owned at least one slave. A rich man might own as many as 500 slaves. An emperor could own as many as 20,000 slaves.

Aqueducts carried water into Rome. Public slaves fixed them so they would always work.

My Life as a Slave

My name is Pallas. I am 12 years old. I am a slave in the household of a rich Roman named Claudius. My mother is a slave, so I am, too.

My mother is a cook. When I was very small, she started teaching me how to work in the kitchen. I cut up vegetables to go with the meat and wash the fruit for dessert. She also taught me how to serve the family. Sometimes I get to carry in food for the main meal of the day.

I am lucky because I am a house slave. I do not have to work in the fields or in the mines. Claudius is not a cruel master but I have to do everything I am told to do by the family. If I do things right, I am not punished.

Sometimes I dream of being free. I would like to go to school and learn to read and write. I hear the family talking about places outside of Rome. I would like to travel and see those places. But I know it will not happen. My master could make me a free person, but there is no reason for him to do that. I am his property. So I try to be happy because I have a place to sleep and food to eat and a mother to take care of me.

"Slavery in Ancient Rome"—Think About It

1. In today's world, who does the work that was done by slaves in ancient Rome?

_____

_____

2. Why was Pallas a slave? What does this tell you about another way people became slaves?

_____

_____

_____

3. What is the difference between a public slave and a private slave?

_____

_____

4. What is a domestic slave? What did they do? Use details from the text to support your answer.

_____

_____

5. Who is giving information in the first part of the text? Who is giving information in the second part? How are they the same? How are they different?

_____

_____

_____

_____

6. What do you think might have been different for a slave working in a Roman home and one working in a mine?

_____

_____

_____

Games Across the Ages

What games do you like to play? Do you like active games, board games, games with lots of people, or games you can play with a few friends? Chances are the games you like to play are the same or similar to games children have played for hundreds, maybe thousands of years (except for computer games, of course).

Children in ancient Greece played many games similar to ones played today. One game they played was **knucklebones**. The modern game **jacks** came from this game. Instead of metal jacks, they used bones of sheep and goats. Later the knucklebones were made from other materials such as metals, ivory, glass, and wood. Knucklebones spread to other countries. It was a common game for children and adults in medieval Britain.

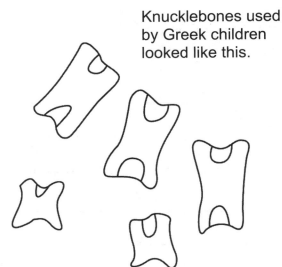

Knucklebones used by Greek children looked like this.

Have you ever played **hopscotch**? Children in medieval England played, too. It was brought to Britain by the **Romans**. Some historians think that hopscotch was invented by Romans as a way to train **soldiers**. The soldiers played wearing their heavy **armor**, jumping through courses that were as long as 98 feet (30 m). Others think that an earlier version of hopscotch was played by the ancient Chinese. Hopscotch is played by children all over the world today.

Maybe you like to play more active games such as **tennis**. Tennis is also a very old game. Tennis started in **medieval** France. It was first played against a wall or over a rope strung in an outside court yard. The ball was hit with the **palm** of the hand. As tennis became more popular, indoor courts were built. The game spread through Europe. Players began using a glove to play, then a solid paddle. Eventually, the modern day **racquet** was invented.

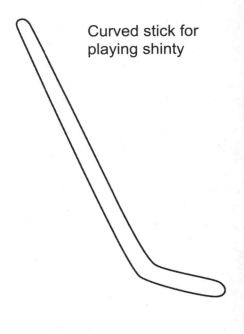

Curved stick for playing shinty

The modern game of ice hockey was first played in North America in 1875. But like many games, similar games were played much earlier. One of these games was **shinty**, played in medieval Britain. The players used curved sticks to hit a leather ball into the goal of the other team. Shinty was played on a grassy field, like field hockey. It was also played in the winter on ice. But using skates to play did not happen until the game came to North America.

18

"Games Across the Ages"—Think About It

1. What is the main topic of the text (the main idea)? What are the four sub-topics?

_____

_____

_____

2. What is armor? How do you know?

_____

_____

_____

3. What was one important difference between shiny played in medieval Britain and ice hockey played in North America?

_____

_____

_____

4. The text says that "Some historians think that hopscotch was invented by Romans as a way to train soldiers." Why do you think they do not know for sure?

_____

_____

_____

5. Why do you think players started wearing gloves to play tennis? How would using a racquet instead of a hand help players play tennis better?

_____

_____

_____

The History of Bicycles

Do you ride a bicycle? Many people ride bikes today for many reasons. Some ride for transportation. Some ride for fun. Some ride for exercise. Riding a modern bicycle is fun and reliable, but this was not always the case.

The bicycle has changed a lot over time. Here are some of these changes.

- The **Draisiennes** was invented around 1816. The bicycle had two wooden wheels, a seat, and handle bars, but no pedals. Riders used their feet to **push** the bicycle along the ground.

- The **vélocipède** was invented around 1867. This bike had **cranks** and pedals attached to the front wheel, like a tricycle. It had a stiff **iron** frame and wooden wheels. This made the ride very **rough**.

- The **Penny Farthing** was invented around 1870. It was all made of **metal** and the wheels were solid **rubber**. The pedals were still attached to the front wheel. The front wheel was much larger than the back wheel, and riders sat up high on the bike. There was no real **braking** system.

- In 1885, John Kemp Starley invented a bike design very similar to the one used today. The seat was between two wheels of the same size. A **sprocket and chain system** attached to pedals drove the bike from the rear wheel. When inflated rubber tires were added, bicycle riding became safe and fun. It was called the safety bicycle.

- Today's bicycles are made of metals such as titanium and carbon. This makes them much lighter. They also have a system of gears that let riders go faster and climb steep hills. There are many types of bikes to choose from. You can buy mountain bikes, road bikes, cruisers, and many more, depending on where and how you want to ride.

Penny Farthing

Design by John Kemp Starley

Bicycle

"The History of Bicycles"—Think About It

1. How was the Draisiennes different from the other bicycles in the text?

_____

_____

2. What do today's bicycles have that the other bicycles did not have. How does this make riding easier?

_____

_____

_____

3. How is this text organized? Does this make it easier or harder to read and understand?

_____

_____

4. The Penny Farthing was not very safe to ride. Why do you think this was true?

_____

_____

_____

5. Draw a timeline of the history of the bicycle. Remember to use dates to show the order of the events. Add important details to describe the bicycles. You can draw your timeline on another piece of paper if you wish.

_____

Our Growing Cities

Over time, most cities get larger.

What Happens?	What Is the Result?
Families who live in a city have children who grow up and need their own places to live. People move to the city from other places.	The city needs more houses, **apartment buildings**, and **condos** for people to live in.
People build new houses, apartment buildings, and condos on green land around the city.	The city gets larger and takes up more land. This is called **urban sprawl**.
Farmland around the city is sold so people can build on it.	There is less farmland in the area for growing food.
When there are fewer farms in an area, more food needs to come from places farther away.	Transporting more food on trucks, trains, and planes puts more **pollution** into the air.
Trees and plants that grew on the green land are **destroyed** when new buildings go up.	Animals that need trees and **plants** for food or shelter must try to find a new place to live.
Some animals will not find a new place to live or food to eat, and they will die.	Animals can become **endangered** or **extinct**.

How Cities Deal with Urban Sprawl

Here are some things cities are doing to stop or slow down the problem of urban sprawl.

- Building houses with smaller backyards: This means more houses can fit on a large piece of land. Then less green land is destroyed for new homes.
- Building taller buildings in a city: Taller buildings provide more spaces for people to live and work inside the city. Many homes can fit on a small patch of land. Then there is less need to put up new buildings on green land.
- Creating greenbelts: A greenbelt is a green area around a city where people are not allowed to build. Only farms, parks, and wild countryside are allowed in a greenbelt, so urban sprawl will not take over the land.

"Our Growing Cities"—Think About It

1. Explain in your own words what *urban sprawl* means.

_____

_____

_____

_____

2. How can urban sprawl lead to more air pollution?

_____

_____

_____

_____

3. How does creating greenbelts save farmland?

_____

_____

_____

_____

4. Think about all the information in the chart. Which structure did the author use to organize the information?

   ☐ Comparison (showing how things are similar and different)

   ☐ Cause and effect (showing how one thing makes one or more things happen)

   ☐ Problem and solution (stating one or more problems and showing how to solve them)

5. Look at the information under the chart. Which structure did the author use to organize the information?

   ☐ Comparison (showing how things are similar and different)

   ☐ Cause and effect (showing how one thing makes one or more things happen)

   ☐ Problem and solution (stating one or more problems and showing how to solve them)

"Our Growing Cities"—Think About It (continued)

6. Why can animals become endangered or extinct as cities grow larger? Use specific details from the text to support your answer.

_____

_____

_____

_____

_____

_____

7. Do you agree with some of the things cities are doing to stop or slow down urban sprawl? Use specific details from the text to support your answer.

_____

_____

_____

_____

_____

_____

8. Is urban sprawl happening in your community? Use specific details from the text to support your answer.

_____

_____

_____

_____

_____

_____

Eating Breakfast

Mornings can be tough. There are lots of things to do to get ready for school, and you have to make sure you get to school on time. Sometimes, kids **skip** breakfast because they do not have time or they do not feel hungry. There are very good reasons to make sure you eat a **healthy** breakfast every day.

Getting Energy

You get energy from the food you eat. After a night's **sleep**, your body needs a **meal** to give you energy to make it through to **lunchtime**. People who do not eat breakfast often have less energy than people who eat a healthy breakfast. Skipping breakfast can make you feel tired during the morning.

Concentrating in School

You need to **concentrate** to pay attention to the teacher and your schoolwork. If you have trouble concentrating, you will find it harder to learn. You might not notice when you are making **mistakes** in your schoolwork. Eating a good breakfast makes it easier to concentrate.

Preventing a Bad Mood

Skipping breakfast can make you **grouchy** during the morning. For many people, this happens because they get hungry before lunchtime, and they cannot eat right away. Being hungry can put you in a **bad mood**.

Getting the Nutrients You Need

Every day, your body needs **nutrients** such as **vitamins** and **minerals**. If you skip breakfast (or any other meal), you might not be giving your body enough of the nutrients it needs to **grow** and stay healthy.

As you can see, there are good reasons to make time for a healthy breakfast every day. It is a great way to get your day off to a good start.

"Eating Breakfast"—Think About It

1. What is the main idea in this text? Explain why you think so.

_____

_____

_____

2. Write a definition for the word _nutrients_. Use details from the text to support your answer.

_____

_____

3. Explain why skipping breakfast can put you in a bad mood.

_____

_____

4. How can eating a healthy breakfast help you do your best in school?

_____

_____

_____

5. a) Which sentence in the text compares two groups of people?

_____

_____

b) Does the comparison show how the two groups are different or similar?

_____

6. Do you agree with the author that eating breakfast is a good idea? Explain.

_____

_____

_____

Why Playing Sports Is Good for You

Playing sports is fun. Even if you do not win every game, you are still spending time doing something you enjoy. Having fun is not the only reason to **get involved** in a sport. Playing sports helps you in many different ways.

Making Your Heart Stronger

Your heart is a **muscle** that **pumps blood** through your body. Like any muscle, your heart gets **stronger** when you make it **work hard**. How do you know when your heart is working hard? You breathe faster. All sports make your heart work harder.

Making New Friends

Playing a sport is a great way to get to know people and make new friends. If you play on a **sports team** at school, you can get to know students in other classes. If you play sports outside of school, you can get to know more kids in your **community**. Some of the people you meet might become new friends.

Learning That Hard Work Pays Off

Playing sports is fun, but it is hard work too. During **practices**, you might do **exercises** and **drills** to **improve** your skills. During a game, you work hard to help your team win. The more you practice and play games, the better you get. This helps you learn that hard work pays off. Learning this important lesson will help you at school and throughout your life.

Improving Self-Esteem

Self-esteem is how you feel about yourself. People with good self-esteem have **confidence** and feel good about themselves. Scientists have discovered that playing sports helps most young people improve their self-esteem. Even if you are not a star player on your team, just being involved in the sport can help you feel better about yourself.

Now you know that there are lots of good reasons to play sports. You will have fun, and you will help yourself in other ways, too.

"Why Playing Sports Is Good for You"—Think About It

1. What is the main idea in this text?

_____

_____

2. List four ideas that the author uses to show that the main idea is true.

_____

_____

_____

_____

3. How are other muscles in your body similar to your heart?

_____

_____

4. Complete the chart to show causes and effects in the text.

Cause	Effect
	Your heart gets stronger.
	You might make new friends in your community.
You work hard at a sport and get better at it.	

5. Write two things that are true of people who have poor self-esteem. (Use clues in the text to help you.)

_____

_____

_____

Turn Down the Music!

Do you turn up the music when a favorite song comes on? That might not be a good idea. Music that is too loud can damage your hearing.

How can loud music damage hearing?

Tiny **nerves** in your ears help you hear. When you listen to loud music for long periods of time, those nerves get damaged, so you will not hear as well. Your body will not be able to repair the nerve damage.

Why are cell phones and portable music players a problem?

Today, people can use **cell phones** and **portable music players** to listen to music through **earphones** anywhere they go. That means people can spend a lot more time listening to music— for example, while riding the bus, walking to school, or shopping. If you like your music loud, spending more time listening to music can lead to hearing problems.

How can you tell if your music is too loud?

When you are using earphones, choose a volume that lets you hear what is going on around you. For example, if you are walking down the street and you cannot hear the traffic, the music is too loud. You also know your music is too loud if people nearby can hear it.

How long can you safely listen to music through earphones?

The answer depends on how loud your music is. If you like very loud music, you might start to damage your hearing after just 10 minutes. If you play music at medium volume, you can safely listen for an hour a day.

Measuring Sound Volume

The volume of sound is measured in **decibels**. The chart below compares the volume of various sounds.

Sounds	Number of Decibels
Normal conversation, a dishwasher	60
A blender, a blow dryer	80
A portable music player at full volume	100
A jet taking off, a police siren	120

"Turn Down the Music!"—Think About It

1. a) What is the structure of this text?
   ☐ Comparison (showing how things are similar and different)
   ☐ Problem and solution (stating one or more problems and showing how to solve them)
   ☐ Question and answer (stating questions and providing the answers)

b) Give evidence to support your answer to the question above.

_____

_____

2. If loud music damages your hearing, will your hearing get better again over time? Why or why not?

_____

_____

_____

_____

3. Before cell phones and portable music players were invented, fewer people damaged their hearing by listening to loud music. Explain why.

_____

_____

_____

4. Why might listening to loud music through earphones be dangerous when you are crossing a street?

_____

_____

5. List the following sounds from loudest to softest: a blow dryer, normal conversation, a police siren, a portable music player at full volume.

_____

_____

When You See Bullying

Many kids would like to help students who get bullied, but the **problem** is that they do not know how to help. Here are some ideas.

1. Tell the bully to stop.

If you silently watch someone get bullied, you might send a **message** to the bully that you think bullying is okay. Be brave and tell the bully to **stop being mean**. If you **speak up** to stop the bullying, you might **encourage** other kids who are watching to speak up too.

2. Help the person who is being bullied.

You might say to the person being bullied, "Come with me. We should go right now." This will show everyone that you are not on the bully's side. If you are in school or in the schoolyard, you can say, "Here comes a teacher!" Even if it is not true, it might **convince** the bully to stop.

3. At another time, talk to the person who was bullied.

Do something to help the person feel better. You could ask the person how they are **feeling** about what happened. Or, you could say, "You do not deserve to be bullied. I hate to see people treated like that."

4. Make sure an adult knows what happened.

Sometimes people who get bullied are afraid to **tell an adult** what happened. They **fear** that if the bully gets in trouble, the situation will get even **worse**. If no one tells an adult, the bully might never stop. It might be up to you to make sure that a teacher, someone else who works at the school, or another adult you **trust** finds out what happened.

Bullying Facts

- About one third of young people say they have been bullied.
- About two thirds of young people who were bullied at school did not tell an adult at the school about it.
- Most bullying happens inside a school, rather than in the schoolyard, or on a school bus, or on the way to school.

"When You See Bullying"—Think About It

1. a) Think about the information in this text. What structure did the author use to organize most of the information?

☐ Comparison (showing how things are similar and different)

☐ Chronology (telling a series of events in the order they happened)

☐ Problem and solution (stating one or more problems and showing how to solve them)

b) Give a reason to support your answer to the question above.

_____

_____

2. If you want to stop a bully, the text says it is okay to say, "Here comes a teacher!" even if it is not true. Do you agree that it is okay to tell a lie in this situation? Explain why or why not.

_____

_____

_____

3. List at least three different text features in this text.

_____

_____

_____

4. Being bullied is a problem that affects many young people. What evidence in the text supports this statement?

_____

_____

5. People who are bullied might fear that telling an adult could make the situation worse. Explain why they might feel this way.

_____

_____

Be a Good Sport!

Sports are more fun for everyone when the players show good **sportsmanship**. Here are some ways to show that you are a good sport.

- **Get involved**. When your teacher, coach, or other kids ask you to get involved in an activity, do not grumble and moan. Show some **enthusiasm** and **get involved**.

- **Be flexible**. People often prefer to play a certain position on a team. For example, if you play hockey, you might prefer being the goalie. If you are asked to play a **different position**, **do not hesitate** to give it a try.

- **Do not be picky about who you play with**. In gym class, your teacher might divide the students into two teams. What if all your friends are on one team, but you get assigned to the other team? Being a good sport means **following instructions** and **not complaining** if you do not like the group you are assigned to.

- **Support your teammates**. Good sportsmanship is about more than just doing your best. It also means encouraging others on your team and celebrating their success when they do well. If a teammate does not do well, **do not criticize**. Instead, say something **supportive** like "Good effort!"

- **Be kind to the other team**. Sports are a form of **competition**. It is easy to decide you do not like the people on the other team just because you are playing against them. Remember that you would not be able to play if you did not have **opponents** to play against. Do not fall into the trap of saying or doing **nasty** things to people on the other team.

- **Control your temper**. Getting angry at the referee, one of the players, or yourself will not help you or your team. Show **respect** for everyone involved in the game, and do not speak disrespectfully to anyone.

- **Do not be a sore loser**. Remember that playing sports is mostly about **having fun**. You can enjoy playing even if your team does not win. Show that you are a **good sport** by **congratulating** the other team when they win.

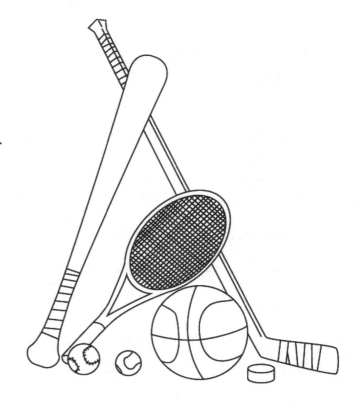

"Be a Good Sport!"—Think About It

1. Does the author believe that winning games is the main goal when you play sports? Use information from the text to support your answer.

_____

_____

_____

_____

2. What does the word *opponents* mean in this text?

_____

_____

_____

3. Does the author believe players should feel thankful toward people on the other team? Use information from the text to support your answer.

_____

_____

_____

_____

4. Which sentence in the text shows that the author believes giving your best effort during a game is one way to be a good sport?

_____

_____

_____

_____

5. People sometimes say that good sportsmanship makes sports more fun for everyone. Do you believe this is true? Give two reasons to support your answer.

_____

_____

_____

_____

_____

_____

6. Create a poster that promotes good sportsmanship.

Fact Sheet: Peer Pressure

Definitions

Peers are people who are about the same age as you. **Peer pressure** is when one or more friends or people your own age make you feel pressured to do something. You feel as though you *have* to do that thing because one or more of your peers are doing it, or are trying to **convince** you to do it.

Positive peer pressure

Positive peer pressure is when you feel pressured to do something good. You might do something that is good for you, good for others, or good for the environment.

Negative peer pressure

Negative, or bad peer pressure is when you feel pressured to do something you shouldn't do. For example, it might be something that **goes against rules**, is dangerous, or is **bad for your health**. It might also be something that goes against your **values**, or what you believe is good or right.

Why peer pressure often works

1) If a friend tries to pressure you to do something, you might feel you should do it to **please** your friend. You might even feel that the person will not be your friend if you do not do it. 2) People often want to fit in with their peers and not feel as though they **stand out** because they are **different** in some way. Sometimes people are afraid others will make fun of them if they do not do what everyone else is doing.

Making decisions when you feel peer pressure

Here are some **questions** to ask yourself when you feel peer pressure to do something:

- Could I get into trouble for doing this?
- Might doing this **hurt myself** or another person, or **hurt someone's feelings**?
- Does this go against my values?
- Will I feel **ashamed** if my family, teachers, or others find out about it?

If you answer "yes" to any of these questions, you are feeling negative peer pressure. Say, "I do not want to do that" and be firm. If people keep pressuring you, say, "I made up my mind. I do not want to talk about it anymore." Then walk away and feel **proud** that you made a **good decision**.

"Fact Sheet: Peer Pressure"—Think About It

1. Leon noticed that most kids at school are wearing a certain type of running shoes. Now he is starting to feel that he should get the same kind of shoes, even though no one has told him he should. Is this an example of peer pressure? Use evidence from the fact sheet to support your answer.

_____

_____

_____

_____

_____

_____

_____

_____

2. Anna and Katya are friends, but Anna's other friends do not like Katya. Anna wants to invite Katya to her birthday party, but Anna's other friends say they will have more fun if Katya is not there. Is this positive or negative peer pressure? Use evidence from the text to support your answer.

_____

_____

_____

_____

_____

_____

_____

"Fact Sheet: Peer Pressure"—Think About It (continued)

3. Write new boldface subheadings that could be used to change the fact sheet into question-and-answer structure.

Subheading in the Text	New Subheading
Definitions	
Positive peer pressure	
Negative peer pressure	
Why peer pressure often works	
Making decisions when you feel peer pressure	

4. Write about a situation of peer pressure you know about. What advice would you give?

_____

_____

_____

_____

_____

_____

The Truth About *Tyrannosaurus Rex*

For a long time, people believed that *Tyrannosaurus rex* (often called *T. rex*) was a fierce predator who had no problem killing its prey.

Then a paleontologist (a scientist who studies fossils) named Jack Horner wondered if *T. rex* was not really a predator at all. He thought this mighty dinosaur might have been a scavenger. Here are some of his reasons:

- Fossils suggest that *T. rex* was too slow and clumsy to be a good predator. Other dinosaurs would find it easy to escape from a *T. rex*.
- A predator needs strong front legs with sharp claws to catch prey. *T. rex's* front legs were very small and had no claws.
- From studying fossils, paleontologists found evidence that *T. rex* had an excellent sense of smell. Scavengers usually have a great sense of smell, which helps them sniff out dead animals to eat.

Many paleontologists disagreed with the idea that *T. rex* was a scavenger. They used the following points to support their opinion:

- Dinosaur predators ate their prey quickly. Most of the time, they would have eaten their prey before a *T. rex* arrived on the scene. A *T. rex* would have had trouble finding enough food as a scavenger.
- *T. rex* did not need strong front legs with claws. It had a huge mouth with sharp teeth and powerful jaws to kill prey.
- Predators need a great sense of smell to track down their prey.

Was *T. rex* a scavenger or a predator? Could fossils answer the question? It turned out that they did. Paleontologists found a fossil of a dinosaur tail that had a broken *T. rex* tooth in it. Had the *T. rex* bitten the dinosaur's tail when the dinosaur was still alive? If so, this would prove that *T. rex* was a predator, not a scavenger. Then the paleontologists saw that the dinosaur's tail bones had started to heal from the *T. rex* bite. This healing would not have happened if the dinosaur were dead when *T. rex* bit it. The fossil provided evidence that *T. rex* was a predator.

Tyrannosaurus rex

"The Truth About *Tyrannosaurus Rex*"—Think About It

1. What is the difference between a predator and a scavenger?

_____

_____

_____

_____

_____

_____

2. The *T. rex* had bitten the dinosaur's tail while the dinosaur was still alive. Why is this evidence that *T. rex* was not a scavenger?

_____

_____

_____

_____

_____

_____

3. Compare how predators and scavengers use their sense of smell.

_____

_____

_____

_____

_____

4. Complete the sentences to write a summary of the text. Use as few words as possible and include only the most important information.

People believed that _____

_____

_____

Then Jack Horner suggested that_____

_____

_____

Many paleontologists _____

_____

_____

Then paleontologists found _____

_____

_____

The new fossil was evidence that *T. rex* was a predator because _____

_____

_____

5. In your opinion, what are two characteristics of a good paleontologist? Explain your thinking.

_____

_____

_____

_____

_____

Where Did the Lions Go?

There are only two kinds of lions in the world today. **Asiatic lions** used to roam from Greece to India. Today, only about 200 to 300 live in a **national park in India**. **African lions** lived in most of **Africa**, except for the desert. Today only 20,000 to 30,000 African lions are found in eastern and southern Africa. What happened?

One of the reasons is loss of habitat. In Africa, lions have lost nearly 75% of their habitat to development. Lions live in **grasslands** and in **wooded areas**. They like to be by **water holes** or **rivers** for drinking. Also many of the animals they hunt come to water to drink. These are areas where people like to live and farm and raise animals. More people means fewer lions.

Lions Need a Lot of Room

Lions are the only members of the **cat family** that live in **groups**. A group of lions living together is called a **pride**. A pride can have from 1 to 4 male lions and 5 to 10 female lions, plus their **cubs**. A pride needs a lot of land. A pride can travel 5 to 6 miles (8 to 10 kilometers) a day hunting.

Prides are very **territorial**. This means that they will fight with any other lions that come into their areas. The fighting usually happens among the male lions. Younger males will **challenge** the male lions of a pride and try to kill them. Then they will take over the pride.

How Can We Save the Lions?

In Africa, most lions are found in **wildlife sanctuaries** and national parks. There are still some who live outside these areas. They are always in danger of being killed by **livestock owners** and **hunters**. Even inside the sanctuaries and parks, lions are not always safe. People need to be **educated** about what is happening to lions and work together to keep them safe.

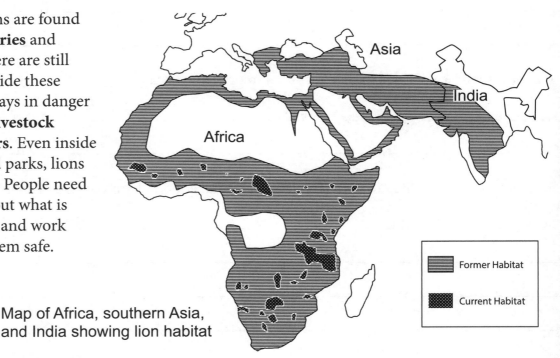

Map of Africa, southern Asia, and India showing lion habitat

"Where Did the Lions Go?"—Think About It

1. Name two kinds of lions in the world today.

_____

_____

2. How are lions different from other wild cats?

_____

_____

3. What is the problem this text talks about?

_____

_____

4. Look at the map. Choose a sentence from the text that you could use as a caption for this map.

_____

_____

5. What do you think sanctuaries are? Why?

_____

_____

6. Why do you think lions never lived in the desert in Africa?

_____

_____

7. Lions are sometimes called Kings of the Jungle. Is this a correct name? Why or why not?

_____

_____

Growing Up

Humans Have Life Stages

Your body has changed a lot since you were a baby. And you will continue to **grow** and **change** as you get older. Scientists and doctors say that humans go through different **life stages**. They have given names and ages to these stages. Not all people go though the stages at the same time. Some grow faster than others; some grow slower. But we all go through the same stages.

A human baby is completely dependent on its mother for the first 2 years of its life.

Life Stages of Humans

Stage	Age	Description
Infant/Toddler	0 to 3 years	• born **helpless** and is completely **dependent** on its mother for food for the first 2 years • learns to **crawl**, then walk • **speaks** in sentences by age 3
Child	4 to 10 years	• learns to take care of itself more and more • starts forming **friendship**s outside of the family
Adolescent	11 to 18 years	• a period of **great growth**; grows taller and heavier • begins to **explore** new **ideas** and **situations**
Adult	18 years and older	• body has **finished** changing and growing

Animals Have Life Stages, Too!

Humans are not the only animals that go through life stages. Some animals have **more simple** life stages. The young are like their parents, but smaller. They have two life stages—young and adult.

They grow to adults quickly, like a pet cat. Some animals have more life stages. They take a longer time to grow. One of these animals is the **orangutan**. Orangutans grow and change as they get older, just like you.

An orangutan baby is completely dependent on its mother for the first 2 years of its life.

Life Stages of Orangutans

Stage	Age	Description
Infant	0 to 4 years	• feeds on its mother's milk for the first 2 years • **stays attached** to its mother constantly for the first 2 years
Juvenile	4 to 8 years	• **independent** of mother but stays in her **territory** • starts to look for their own food
Adolescent	Female: 8 to 15 years Male: 8 to 13 years	• female makes contact with other adolescent females • male is independent and moves into new territories • male **socializes** with adolescent males and females
Sub-adult	Male only: 13 to 18 years	• socializes less and spends more and more time alone • still growing; not a full-sized male yet
Adult	Female: 15 years and older Male: 18 years and older	• female starts to have babies and lives with her babies • male lives alone

In the life stages of the orangutan, the juvenile stage is the same as the child stage in humans.

"Growing Up"—Think About It

1. Do all humans go through the same life stages? What might be different for some humans?

_____

_____

_____

_____

2. What is one difference between the life stages of a human and the life stages of a cat?

_____

_____

_____

3. What is this text comparing? How do the charts help you compare?

_____

_____

_____

4. Orangutans have one more life stage than humans. What is this stage? What is unusual about this stage?

_____

_____

_____

5. What is the same about the child stage of humans and the juvenile stage of orangutans? What is different?

_____

_____

_____

Habitat Communities

What Is a Community?

The word **community** can mean a group of people together in one place. Your **neighborhood** is a community. The people in your neighborhood all live in the same area.

Depending on Each Other

People in communities **depend** on one another. Think of your **school community**. Students need teachers to teach them. **Teachers** need **students** to teach. **Principals** make sure their schools run smoothly. Principals need everyone else to help. The people in your school community need each other.

Plants and animals make communities, too.

Habitat Communities

A **habitat community** is made up of all the plants and animals that live in a particular habitat. They depend on each other.

Animals in a community need the plants. Plants provide some animals with **food**. They provide **places to hide**. They also provide **homes**.

Plants in a community need the animals. Animal **droppings fertilize** the soil. This helps plants grow. Bees move **pollen** between flowers while they eat. This helps plants produce **seeds** and **fruit**.

Some animals depend on other animals for food. For example, mice provide food for owls.

Why Habitat Communities Are Important

What if all the trees **disappeared** from a habitat? Plants would not have shady places to grow. Birds' nests would be on the ground. **Predators** could eat birds' eggs.

Imagine that all the mice disappeared. Animals that eat mice might not find enough food to **survive**.

Every living thing in a habitat community depends on each other. They help each other to survive. They may not survive without each other.

"Habitat Communities"—Think About It!

1. How is a habitat community similar to your school community? Use information from the text and your own ideas

_____

_____

_____

_____

2. Which is more important in a habitat community—animals or plants? Or are animals and plants equally important? Give reasons for your answer.

_____

_____

_____

_____

3. What is the main idea of this text? Explain your thinking.

_____

_____

_____

_____

4. What is the relationship between plants and animals in a habitat community?

_____

_____

_____

How Does That Help?

Humans are one of the few animals that can live anywhere in the world. Most animals live in a particular place or **habitat**. They get everything they need to live from their habitat. Polar bears live in the Arctic, mostly on the ice in the ocean. Living on the ice keeps them close to their food source—seals.

Animals have different **physical features** that help them live in their habitat. One feature of the **polar bear** is long, **stiff hair** on the pads of its feet. These hairs help keep the bear's feet warm on the cold ice. They also help the bear from slipping on the ice. These physical features are called **structural adaptations**.

There are many, many interesting structural adaptations that help animals survive.

Maned wolf

The Maned Wolf

The **maned wolf** is not really a wolf, but it is part of the same **family** as dogs, wolves, and foxes. It lives in the tall **grasslands** of South America. This predator eats small birds and animals, but it also eats a lot of fruit. It has a special adaptation. The maned wolf has very **long legs**, like the legs of a deer. They help it see over the tall grass to look for **prey**.

The Camel

Dromedary camels are the camels that have one hump on their backs. They are often called **Arabian camels**. These camels live in the **desert** in places such as North Africa. These deserts are mostly sand. Camels have two special **adaptations** to protect them from blowing sand. They have two rows of long **eyelashes** to help keep the sand from getting in their eyes. They can also close their **nostrils** to keep out the blowing sand.

Dromedary camel

Penguins

Penguins live beside the ocean in places such as Antarctica, New Zealand, Galapagos, and South America. Penguins are birds but they **cannot fly**. Their wings have become more like **flippers**. Flippers help make them **excellent swimmers**. This is good because they get their food from the ocean around them. The only time they are in danger from **predators** is when they are in the water. Penguins are white on the front and black on the back. In the water, they cannot be easily seen from below because their white fronts **blend** with the lighter surface of the water. They cannot be easily seen from above because their dark backs blend with the darkness of the water below.

Penguin

"How Does That Help?"—Think About It

1. What is a habitat? What do animals get from a habitat?

_____

_____

_____

_____

2. Describe in your own words one structural adaptation of each animal in the text. Tell how the structural adaptation helps each animal.

a) polar bear

_____

_____

b) maned wolf

_____

_____

c) camel

_____

_____

d) penguin

_____

_____

3. Why do you think a polar bear is white?

_____

_____

4. Think about polar bears and penguins that live in Antarctica. What is the same about them? What is different?

_____

_____

_____

_____

_____

_____

5. What is a predator? How do you know?

_____

_____

_____

_____

_____

_____

6. Imagine walking across a huge desert full of sand. Describe two structural adaptations camels would need to help them do this. These may be adaptations that you know about or adaptations that you think they should have.

_____

_____

_____

_____

_____

_____

Producers, Consumers, and Decomposers

Every living thing needs energy to live. Scientists group living things into three **categories**, based on how they get energy. Those categories are producers, consumers, and decomposers.

Producers

Producers use the **energy** in **sunlight** to make their own food. Most producers are **green plants**. They use a process called **photosynthesis** to make food from sunlight. Grasses, bushes, and trees are all examples of producers.

Consumers

Consumers get their energy from eating other **living things**. Lions, skunks, rabbits, and spiders are all consumers. Animals such as rabbits that eat only plants are called **herbivores**. Animals such as lions that eat only animals are called **carnivores**. Animals such as skunks that eat plants and other animals are called **omnivores**.

Decomposers

Decomposers eat **dead** plants and animals to get energy. When living things die, their bodies still contain many **nutrients**. Decomposers help to **break down**, or **decompose**, a dead plant or animal. When something that was alive decomposes, nutrients from the plant or animal go back into the soil. Then plants can use these nutrients to help them grow. Mushrooms, worms, and **bacteria** are examples of decomposers.

Food Chains

A **food chain** shows how animals in a habitat get energy from each other. Below is an example of a food chain in a **forest habitat**.

A grasshopper gets energy by eating grass.

Grass uses energy in sunlight to make food. Nutrients from the hawk's body that are in the soil also help it grow.

A snake gets energy by eating grasshoppers.

The hawk dies and bacteria get energy by feeding on it. Nutrients from the hawk's body go into the soil.

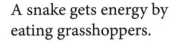

A hawk swoops down and gets energy by eating a snake.

"Producers, Consumers, and Decomposers"—Think About It

1. What structure does the author use to organize most of the information in this text?
- ☐ Problem and solution (stating one or more problems and showing how to solve them)
- ☐ Chronology (telling a series of events in the order they happened)
- ☐ Classification (grouping things into categories)

2. A Venus flytrap is a green plant that eats flies. Explain why this plant is a producer even though is consumes flies.

_____

_____

_____

3. Which categories of consumers eat producers?

_____

_____

4. Explain how decomposers help plants. Use details from the text to support your answer.

_____

_____

5. How does the diagram help you understand what a food chain is?

_____

_____

_____

6. Write each living thing in the food chain in the correct column below.

Producer	Consumer	Decomposer

Deforestation

Deforestation happens when people cut down all the **trees** in a large area of a forest and do not plant new trees. Large parts of our planet were once covered with forests. In the last 200 years, about half of these forests have been cut down.

Reasons for Deforestation

- People need trees to make **lumber** for **construction projects** and various kinds of **paper products**. In parts of the world where people do not have electricity, wood is used for heating homes and cooking.

- Farmers need more land for planting crops and raising animals.

- As cities grow larger, more space is needed for building homes, stores, and factories.

- The land under a forest may contain valuable natural resources, such as oil, natural gas, or minerals. People deforest the land so they can mine these underground natural resources.

What Happens When Forests Are Destroyed

- Forest trees protect the soil from the heat of the sun. The **roots** of trees help to **hold** the soil in place. When forests are destroyed, the soil dries out and there are no roots to hold the soil in place. Then rain can **erode**, wash away, the soil.

- Forests provide a habitat for many different types of plants and animals. When forests are destroyed, some plants and animals can become **endangered** or **extinct**.

- **Carbon dioxide** is a gas in the air that leads to climate change. Plants absorb carbon dioxide and give off **oxygen**. When forests are destroyed, more carbon dioxide remains in the air and makes climate change worse.

54

"Deforestation"—Think About It

1. How could reusing and recycling wood and paper products help animals?

_____

_____

_____

_____

_____

2. Use information from the text to give one reason why climate change was not a big problem 200 years ago.

_____

_____

_____

_____

3. What information in the text explains why it might be difficult for new trees to grow in an area that was deforested?

_____

_____

_____

_____

_____

4. If we stop cutting down any trees, some people would lose their jobs. Use information in the text to list at least three examples of types of jobs that might be lost.

_____

_____

_____

_____

A Sound Experiment

Sound is **invisible**. We cannot see it. But we can do experiments to see and feel what it does. Here is an **experiment** a Grade 4 class did to learn what sound does to the **air** around it.

Materials

- scissors
- plastic bottle
- plastic bag
- elastic band
- tea light candle

Steps

Do the steps in order.

1. Have an adult cut off the bottom end of the bottle using the scissors.
2. Cut a piece from the plastic bag so it is larger than the bottle bottom. Cover the bottom of the bottle with it. Make sure the plastic is tight.
3. Stretch the elastic band over the the bottom of the bottle to hold the plastic in place.
4. Light the tea light candle.
5. Point the top end of the bottle toward the tea light candle. Hold it about 1 inch (2.5 centimeters) from the flame.
6. Tap the piece of plastic at the end of the bottle with your fingertips.

Bottle

Plastic bag

Elastic band

Tea light candle

What Happens?

The candle flame goes out.

Why It Happens

The sound from the **tapping** makes the **air molecules** on the other side of the plastic **vibrate**. These vibrations make the air molecules next to them vibrate. These vibrations move through the bottle and out the other end and blow out the candle.

"A Sound Experiment"—Think About It

1. Why can we not see sound?

_____

_____

_____

2. What can we learn about sound by doing experiments?

_____

_____

_____

3. Draw a diagram of Step 5. Label the parts of the diagram.

4. What are air *molecules*? Explain your thinking.

_____

_____

_____

5. Explain how the experiment works in your own words.

_____

_____

_____

_____

6. Do you think this experiment would work in a vacuum? (A vacuum is a space without air.) Why or why not?

_____

_____

_____

_____

7. Why is it important to do the steps of an experiment in the order they are written?

_____

_____

_____

How Hard Is That?

Our world is full of rocks. They are everywhere. Rocks can be as big as a **mountain** or as small as a **grain of sand**.

There are many types of rocks. All rocks are made up of two or more **minerals**. There are about 4,000 minerals on Earth. Different minerals can combine to make different rocks. That is one of the reasons there are so many types of rocks.

Each mineral is made up of one **substance**. If you cut a mineral into pieces, each piece would look the same throughout. If you cut a rock into pieces, each piece would look different. Some minerals that you might know are **gold**, **copper**, and **quartz**.

Properties of Minerals

It is not always easy to tell the difference between minerals. People who study minerals use **properties** or **characteristics** to identify them. Some properties they use are

- color   • **luster**, or how shiny they look in light   • **hardness**
- **transparency**, or how much light shines through them

Here, we will talk about mineral hardness.

Hardness

Some minerals are very hard; others are very soft. The **Mohs Hardness Scale** is used to **compare** the hardness of any mineral. The scale lists 10 common minerals from softest (1) to hardest (10). Each mineral can only **scratch** the minerals that have a lower number than it on the scale.

You can use the minerals on the scale to test other minerals for hardness. For example, **talc** is the softest (number 1). If you used talc to scratch another mineral and it left a mark, then the mineral is softer than talc. If it did not leave a mark, then it is harder than talc. Diamond is the hardest (number 10). Diamonds will scratch almost any other mineral.

You can also test the hardness of minerals using other things. The chart below tells how to test to find out where a mineral fits on the scale from 1 to 6 using everyday tools.

Mohs Hardness Scale
1 Talc
2 Gypsum
3 Calcite
4 Fluorite
5 Apatite
6 Feldspar
7 Quartz
8 Topaz
9 Corundum
10 Diamond

Scale	Description
1	can be scratched easily with your fingernail; crumbles
2	can be scratched with your fingernail
3	can be scratched with a copper penny
4	can be scratched easily with a nail or a pocket knife
5	can be scratched with a nail or a pocket knife
6	can be scratched with a steel file

"How Hard Is That?"—Think About It

1. What are rocks made from?

_____

2. What is one reason that there are so many different kinds of rocks? Explain your answer.

_____

_____

_____

_____

3. If you cut a piece of a mineral into two parts, what would each part look like?

_____

_____

_____

_____

4. How could you measure the transparency of something? Name one thing that is very transparent.

_____

_____

_____

_____

5. If you had a mineral that was a number 5 on the Mohs Hardness Scale, which minerals could it scratch?

_____

_____

_____

_____

6. The mineral fluorite is number 4 on the Mohs Hardness Scale. You use it to scratch another mineral. No mark was left on the other mineral. What does this tell you about the other mineral?

_____

_____

_____

_____

7. Imagine you have found a mineral. You rub it with your finger and little pieces rub off. What would be the number of this mineral on the Mohs Hardness Scale? Why?

_____

_____

_____

_____

8. You are testing a mineral for hardness. You can scratch it with a nail but you need to press quite hard. What would be the number of this mineral on the Mohs Hardness Scale?

_____

_____

_____

_____

9. What does this text make you wonder about?

_____

_____

_____

_____

Magnets Are More Than Fun

Have you ever played with magnets? Then you know that a magnet will **pull** some objects toward it. Magnets do this because they make an invisible area called a **magnetic field**. It is this magnetic field that makes magnets **attract** objects made from some **metals**. Metals that magnets will attract are **iron**, **nickel**, and **cobalt**. Magnets will not attract objects made from most other metals, such as gold, silver, or copper.

Bar magnets have two poles, or ends. One end is the **north pole**. The other end is the **south pole**. Have you tried putting two bar magnets together? If you put the north end of one magnet close to the south end of the other magnet, the magnets will attract each other. If you put the south poles together or the north poles together, the magnets will repel or push away from each other.

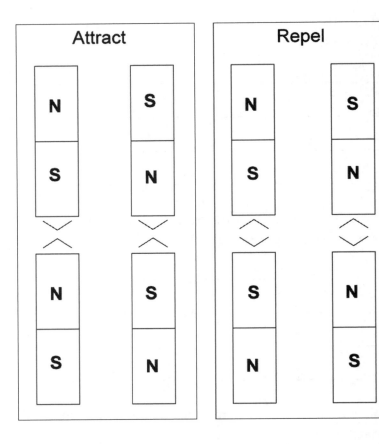

Earth's Magnetic Field

Earth also makes a magnetic field. Scientists believe this happens because the **center** of Earth is made of **melted iron** and **nickel**. This makes a big magnet with one end at the North Pole and the other end at the South Pole.

Earth's magnetic field helps us find **directions** on Earth. A magnetic **compass** has a **needle**. When this needle can move freely, it will point to the North Pole of Earth. Then you can figure out the other directions.

Scientists believe that the poles of Earth have **switched** in the past. So if you were alive 800,000 years ago, the compasses we use today would have pointed to the South Pole.

Earth's magnetic field also protects us from **solar wind**. Solar wind comes from the Sun. It has **particles** in it that can harm living things on Earth. Earth's magnetic field protects us by repelling these particles.

"Magnets Are More Than Fun"—Think About It

1. What is a magnetic field? What does a magnetic field do?

_____

_____

_____

2. What happens when two south poles of a bar magnet are put together?

_____

_____

_____

3. Use what you know about magnets to explain the phrase "opposites attract".

_____

_____

_____

4. How does Earth's magnetic field help us?

_____

_____

5. Do you think a magnet would attract an object made from glass? Why or why not?

_____

_____

6. Why does a needle in a magnetic compass need to move freely?

_____

_____

_____

A Star Is Born

We need light to see. Light can be **natural** (from nature) or **artificial** (made by people). The most important source of natural light is our Sun. Our Sun makes its own light just like all stars in the sky. But where do stars come from?

A Star Nursery

Stars are born in a star nursery called a **nebula**. Stars are made from **gases** and **dust**. In the nebula, the gases and dust come together to form a **core**, or center. The core gets bigger and bigger, and the baby star gets hotter and hotter. When it is hot enough, the star begins to burn a gas called **hydrogen**. It is the burning of hydrogen that produces **light**, **heat**, and **energy**.

Stars Get Older

These baby stars grow, just like you do. Some stars are smaller than others. Our Sun is an average-sized star, called a **yellow dwarf** star. These stars give off light that is white to light yellow. This light becomes brighter as the stars get older.

Smaller stars last longer than bigger stars. Yellow dwarf stars can last for 10 billion years. Then they start to get bigger. The **temperature** gets **cooler** and the light they give off looks red. They become **red giant** stars.

Our Sun is about halfway through its life, so it will not become a red giant for billions of years yet.

The End of a Star

Near the end of its life, a red giant star will collapse and become much, much smaller. It will also get much cooler and the light it gives off will not be very bright. It is now a **white dwarf** star. In time, white dwarf stars become **invisible** because they give off so little light.

The Life of a Star

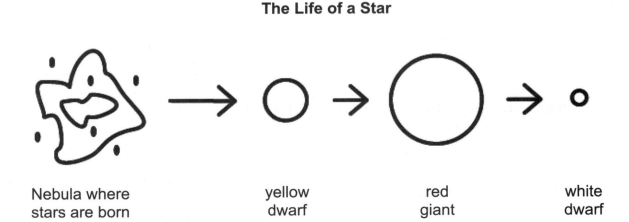

Nebula where stars are born   yellow dwarf   red giant   white dwarf

"A Star Is Born"—Think About It

1. What is the difference between natural light and artificial light? What are some examples of natural light? What are some examples of artificial light?

_____

_____

_____

_____

2. What are stars made from?

_____

_____

_____

3. What happens to a baby star as its core gets bigger?

_____

_____

_____

4. How does our Sun produce light?

_____

_____

_____

5. Think about a yellow dwarf, a red giant, and a white dwarf star.

a) Describe the light produced by each of these stars.

_____

_____

_____

b) Describe the temperature of each of these stars.

_____

_____

_____

c) Describe the size of each of these stars.

_____

_____

_____

6. How is the life of a star such as our Sun similar to the life of a person? How is it different?

_____

_____

_____

_____

7. About how many years will it take before our Sun starts to become a red giant?

_____

8. What does this text make you wonder about?

_____

_____

_____

_____

Seeing Stars

If you look up at a clear night sky when you are far away from cities, you will probably see over 2,000 stars. If you look at the night sky when you are in the middle of a large city, you might see only 10 stars. Why?

Stars shine **constantly**. We see them only at night because they are **brighter** than the night sky. The daytime sky is very bright, so no stars are **visible**. Why can you not see a lot of stars from a large city at night? All the city lights makes the night sky brighter. We see only the stars that shine brighter than the night sky.

Light Pollution

Many cities create much more light at night than people really need. Bright, **flashing billboards** and **store signs** create light when most people are at home sleeping. Some **office buildings** keep the lights on all night. Light that we do not really need is called **light pollution**. Without light pollution, people could see many more stars from cities.

How important is it to see lots of stars at night? For **astronomers**, it is very important. They use telescopes in **observatories** to study stars. Some observatories were built many years ago, in places far away from bright lights. Over time, cities have been created close to some of these observatories. As the cities grow, they create more light pollution. Then astronomers at the observatories can see fewer stars.

Reducing Light Pollution Is Not Just About Seeing Stars

People who want to reduce light pollution point out that turning off **unnecessary** lights at night means people **save money** on electricity. **Generating electricity** can create **air pollution**, so using less electricity for light is good for the **environment**. One astronomer gives another reason for reducing light pollution. "I believe every child should have a chance to see the night sky filled with thousands of stars," she said. "It helps them understand that we are part of a huge universe that is amazing and, in many ways, still a **fascinating mystery**."

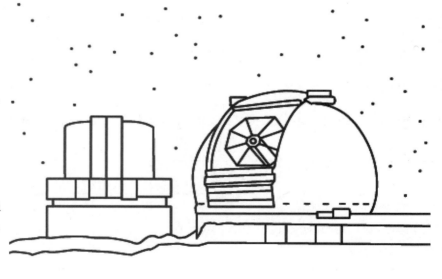

An observatory

"Seeing Stars"—Think About It

1. Explain why people see fewer stars when they are in a large city than they do when they are in a place far away from cities.

_____

_____

_____

2. People who live in a small town might see about 200 stars at night. Why do they see more stars than people who live in a large city?

_____

_____

_____

3. Use information in the text to define the word *astronomer*.

_____

_____

4. Some observatories are built on very small islands, far out in the ocean. Why are these islands good locations for an observatory?

_____

_____

_____

5. What information in the text tells you that astronomers still have lots to learn about the universe?

_____

_____

6. How can reducing light pollution be good for our planet?

_____

_____

The World at Night

It is late at night. You are sound asleep in your bed. The only light outside is coming from the moon and a few streetlights. It seems like the whole world around you is asleep. But is it?

Animals at Night

There are many things happening outside at night. Many animals **move** around and **feed** while we sleep. These animals are called **nocturnal** animals. You may see some nocturnal animals during daylight, but most spend the day resting and sleeping.

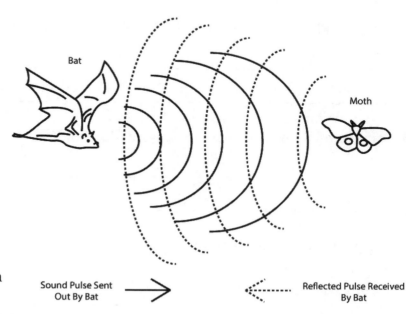

Nocturnal animals use all their **senses** when they are out at night. But some senses are more **important** than others. Some animals, such as **owls**, can see very well at night. They have excellent **eyesight**. **Field mice** and **coyotes** have an excellent sense of **smell** that helps them find food at night. **Red foxes** and **skunks** depend a lot on their **hearing**.

Bats use sound to find their way around at night and **catch insects** to eat. They send out **high-pitched sounds** that bounce off nearby objects. They hear the **echoes** and use them to figure out where the objects are. Bats can do something special to help them do this. Their ears have **flaps**. The flaps cover their ears when they first make the sounds, and uncover them after. This way the bats know which sound is the one they are sending out and which sound is the one bouncing back.

Many insects such as moths, fireflies, mosquitoes, and crickets are nocturnal. Some people think all nocturnal insects are attracted to light. Some insects such as moths, are attracted by light, but many are not—they avoid light.

Plants at Night

Plants are also very **active** at night. During the day, they use **sunlight** to make their own **food**. At night, they change the food they make into **energy** to grow. Some plants only **bloom** at night. During the day, their flowers are **closed**. And some plants only release their **scent**, or smell, after the sun goes down.

"The World at Night"—Think About It

1. What are nocturnal animals? Name three nocturnal animals?

_____

_____

2. What do plants do during the day? What do plants do at night?

_____

_____

3. Some animals are nocturnal. Some are **diurnal.** What do you think *diurnal* means? Why?

_____

_____

4. Use your own words to describe how a bat finds food at night. Tell what happens in the order it happens.

_____

_____

_____

_____

_____

5. Complete the diagram below. Think about the text and complete the graphic organizer below.

Main idea:
_____

Subheading 1: _____

Detail: _____

_____

Subheading 2: _____

Detail: _____

_____

Earthquake!

Read the two **reports** about an **earthquake** in California in 1989. The first report is by someone who **experienced** the earthquake. The second report is a news report by someone who did not experience the earthquake.

Report 1: Caught in an Earthquake

I had left work a little earlier than usual and was at the mall, browsing in a store. Suddenly there was a huge **bang**, followed by the most **incredible noise**, like hundreds of airplanes flying overhead. I had no idea what was happening. I did not even think about an earthquake, but then everything started **shaking**. Lights hanging from the ceiling were **swaying**, and things started falling off the store shelves. I was so **startled** that for a second I just **froze**. Then the lights went out.

I realized that it was an earthquake and I wanted to get out of the mall fast. Everyone in the mall started **rushing** to get outside. It is really hard to walk or run when the floor is shaking, it is dark, and everyone is in a **panic** to get out. I do not know if people were shouting or screaming because there was so much other noise. The earth kept **rumbling**, windows were **breaking**, and the whole building was making loud **creaking** sounds.

By the time I got outside, the rumbling and shaking had stopped. I sat down on the ground. At first, there was just **silence**. All these people who had rushed out of the mall were standing around completely silent. I guess we were all so **astonished** by what had happened. Next, a child started crying, then there was more crying, people shouting, lots of noise.

I started walking to my home a few blocks away. The streets were full of people because nobody wanted to be indoors. Everyone was in shock and sidewalks were covered with broken glass. Some older buildings had **collapsed** into piles of **rubble**. The sidewalk was all broken up and I kept tripping. I was so relieved to discover that my home was not **destroyed**.

Report 2: Earthquake Rocks San Francisco Area

A powerful earthquake lasting about 15 seconds hit California yesterday. Nine people have been reported **killed** and hundreds of **injured** people crowded hospital **emergency** rooms. One **bridge** and a raised section of **highway** collapsed during the earthquake.

The number of people killed and injured is expected to rise as **rescuers** search collapsed buildings. Thousands of people have been left **homeless** because their homes collapsed or are now too badly **damaged** to enter.

Earthquake! (continued)

Many **communities** were left without **power**, which caused **traffic jams** after traffic lights stopped working. Traffic problems could have been much worse, since the quake hit at 5:04 p.m. when many people are normally on their way home from work. However, officials believe that many had left work early to watch the World Series baseball game scheduled at San Francisco's Candlestick Park. Some fans waiting at the **stadium** for the game to start were thrown from their seats when the earthquake struck.

Ambulance workers report that most of the people they have treated are suffering from shock and cuts. Some city streets are **littered** with bricks and shards of broken glass, which will take days for city workers to clean up.

Buildings and roadways in California are supposed to be constructed to survive a powerful earthquake. California experiences thousands of earthquakes every year, but most are so weak that they pass unnoticed.

Area Affected by the Earthquake

The worst damage happened in areas close to the center of the earthquake.

"Earthquake!"—Think About It

1. a) Which report uses chronological structure (telling events in the order in which they happened)?   ☐ Report 1   ☐ Report 2

b) Which report starts by stating the main idea?   ☐ Report 1   ☐ Report 2

2. a) Which report does the best job of helping you understand how people felt during and after the earthquake?   ☐ Report 1   ☐ Report 2

b) Use the report you chose above. Write two details from the report that say how people felt.

_____

_____

_____

_____

3. a) Which report tells you about people who were killed or injured?   ☐ Report 1   ☐ Report 2

b) Use the report you chose above. Write two details from the report that help you learn more about people who were killed or injured.

_____

_____

_____

_____

4. Write two facts people can learn from the map that are not in the text of either report.

_____

_____

_____

_____

5. If you are indoors during an earthquake, people say it is safer to stay indoors and hide under a table until the shaking stops. Use details from Report 1 to explain why it can be dangerous to try to get outside.

_____

_____

_____

_____

_____

_____

_____

_____

6. What advice would you give to someone who is in an earthquake? Use information from the text and your own ideas.

_____

_____

_____

_____

_____

_____

_____

_____

What Does a Marine Biologist Do?

Marine Biologists

Biologists study living things, including **plants** and **animals**. A **marine biologist** is someone who studies plants and animals that live in the **ocean**. Thousands of different plants and animals live in the ocean, so many marine biologists choose to study just one thing. For example, a marine biologist might decide to study dolphins, sharks, or seaweed.

Where Marine Biologists Do Their Work

Some marine biologists work on a **boat**. They might watch whales that come to the ocean's surface and observe how they behave and where they travel. Marine biologists might also use **underwater cameras** to watch animals that do not come to the surface.

Other marine biologists go down into the ocean. Some are **scuba divers** who **collect** underwater plants so they can learn more about them. The scuba divers might also collect marine animals. They **study** the animals to learn about how their bodies work and whether they have any **diseases**.

Sometimes marine biologists use a small type of **submarine** to go into the ocean. The submarine has bright lights and lots of clear plastic so people can see what is happening under the ocean's surface.

Some marine biologists work in **laboratories**, observing fish in large water tanks, or looking at tiny sea creatures under a microscope.

Becoming a Marine Biologist

If you are interested in becoming a marine biologist, learn to read and write well. Marine biologists read and write many **scientific reports**. You should also work hard at science. People take lots of science **courses** at a **university** to become marine biologists.

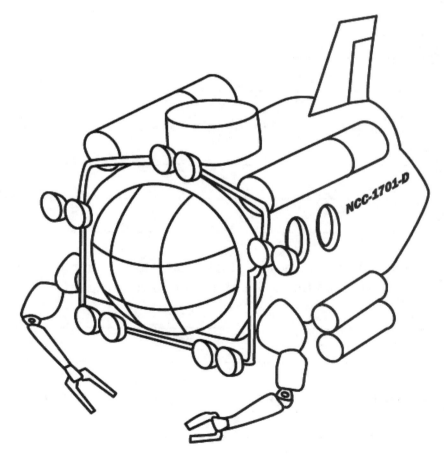

This small submarine has lots of lights for seeing things in deep water, and claws for picking things up off the ocean floor.

"What Does a Marine Biologist Do?"—Think About It

1. Write a definition for marine animals.

_____

_____

2. Different types of scientists often become experts in one particular topic. Is this true of marine biologists? Give evidence from the text to support your answer.

_____

_____

_____

3. Some marine biologists do not go down into the ocean. What are three examples of ways these marine biologists study animals?

_____

_____

_____

4. Scuba divers and small submarines cannot stay underwater for very long periods of time. Why?

_____

_____

_____

5. The illustration shows a small submarine that marine biologists might use. Write two things you learned about this submarine from the illustration.

_____

_____

6. What is one way that marine biologists share the information they learn?

_____

_____

What Does a Carpenter Do?

A carpenter uses tools to join together pieces of wood to build **structures**.

Getting Started

Before carpenters can start building, they need to have a **plan** to follow. The plan is a **diagram** of the structure they are going to build. The diagram gives all the **measurements** of the structure. Carpenters use the plan to figure out how much wood they will need, what size and shape each piece of wood needs to be, and what tools will be needed.

Battery-powered drill

Building with Tools

Carpenters use **power tools** and **hand tools**. Power tools get their power from **electricity**. Examples of power tools are electric saws, drills, and sanders. Hand tools do not use electricity. Carpenters use their **muscles** for power when they use hand tools such as hammers and hand saws.

Types of Carpenters

Carpenters are divided into different categories, depending on the type of work they do. **Construction carpenters** work on building large structures, such as new homes, office buildings, and stores. **Residential carpenters** work on homes that have already been built. They might put new wood floors in a house, repair the roof, or add a deck to the back of the house. **Furniture makers** build different types of wooden furniture. For example, if you want new kitchen cupboards, a bookshelf, or a table, a furniture maker can make what you need in the exact size and shape that you want.

Handsaw

Skills

Here are some examples of skills that carpenters need:
- **Math** skills: Carpenters use math skills when they add, subtract, multiply, or divide different measurements.
- **Safety** skills: Carpenters need to know how to use tools safely.
- **Drawing** skills: When furniture makers **design** a new piece of furniture, they make a drawing to show the **customer** what it will look like.

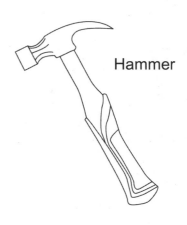

Hammer

"What Does a Carpenter Do?"—Think About It

1. All carpenters use nails, screws, and glue. Why are these materials important in any carpenter's job?

_____

_____

2. The text mentions electric saws, drills, and sanders. Why did the author provide these examples of tools?

_____

3. Power tools need electricity to work. Hand tools also need a source of energy to do work. Where does this energy come from?

_____

4. Which type of carpenter would you need for each of the projects below?

Building a bridge: _____

Replacing a home's old stairs: _____

5. The word _residential_ comes from the word _residence_. Use information from the text to help you write a definition of residence.

_____

_____

6. How is putting together a wooden bookshelf from a store similar to and different from a furniture maker's job?

Similar: _____

_____

Different: _____

_____

What Does a Firefighter Do?

A firefighter does much more than just put out fires. Find out about some of the different activities firefighters do and what skills they need.

Activities of a Firefighter

Along with fires, firefighters rush to **emergencies** such as serious traffic accidents, explosions, and train and airplane crashes. Firefighters are often the first people at an emergency. They help people and animals **escape** if they are **trapped**. They also give **first aid** to injured people until an **ambulance** arrives. Firefighters stay at the scene until they are sure there is no more danger.

An important part of firefighting is **being prepared** for an emergency. Firefighters exercise to **stay fit** and **practice** using firefighting equipment effectively. Firefighters also **check** the **fire engine** and all their **equipment** to make sure everything is in good shape and works properly.

Firefighters work with people in the **community** to help **prevent fires** and keep people safe. Firefighters often **visit schools** and **businesses** to make sure people know what to do if there is a fire. Sometimes a firefighter will visit people's homes to check for any dangerous **fire hazards**.

Skills a Firefighter Needs

Here are some of the skills that firefighters use on the job:

- **Decision-making skills**: Firefighters need to be able to make good decisions quickly in **stressful situations**. For example, a firefighter needs to decide when it is too dangerous to enter a burning building.
- **Teamwork skills**: Firefighters work in teams, so they need good teamwork skills. For example, a firefighter needs to be able to **follow instructions** from the **team leader**.
- **Speaking and writing skills**: Firefighters sometimes give **oral presentations** to the public. After an emergency, they write reports about what happened and what they did.

"What Does a Firefighter Do?"—Think About It

1. What is the main idea of the text?

_____

_____

2. What examples does the author use to help readers understand the types of emergencies firefighters go to?

_____

_____

3. What are three things firefighters do to make sure they are ready for an emergency?

_____

_____

_____

_____

4. Use information in the text to help you write a definition of _fire hazard_.

_____

_____

5. What example in the text shows that firefighters need to look after their own safety?

_____

_____

6. Firefighters need to have good knowledge of the streets and roads in their community. Give two reasons why this is important.

_____

_____

_____

_____

Roald Dahl

Have you read *Charlie and the Chocolate Factory*? Or *James and the Giant Peach*? If you have, you are one of thousands of children who have read stories by Roald Dahl.

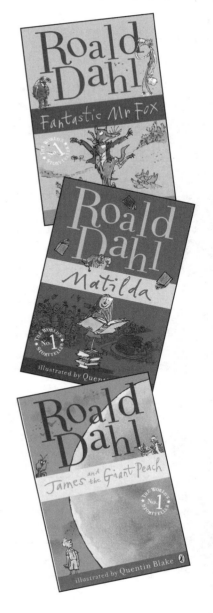

Mr. Dahl is one of the most-read authors of children's books. Many of his stories have been made into movies, like *Fantastic Mr. Fox* and *The Witches*. His book *Matilda* has been made into a **musical play**. And it is not just children who like his work. Adults do too. Maybe that is why there is an official **Roald Dahl day** that happens on his birthday every year.

Mr. Dahl had a very interesting life. He was born in 1916. After finishing school in England, he lived in many different places such as Newfoundland, Tanzania, Africa, and Washington, DC. He was a **fighter pilot** in World War II. He wrote stories for adults. Many of these were published in **magazines**. But he is best known for his children's stories.

Maybe Mr. Dahl's mother was one of the reasons he became a writer of children's books. She told him and his sisters stories when they were young. He loved the tales about **trolls** and other **strange creatures**. When he was older, he loved **adventure stories**.

Mr. Dahl did not write any of his famous books for children until he had children of his own. He used to tell his children stories, just like his mother did with him. Then he started to write them. He thought that he was good at writing these stories because he could see the world through children's eyes.

He said, "If you want to remember what it is like to live in a **child's world**, you've got to get down on your hands and knees and live like that for a week. You'll find you have to look up at all these… giants around you who are always telling you what to do and what not to do."

Mr. Dahl also thought it was important for children to read. He knew that stories had to keep his readers interested. He said, "I have a **passion** for teaching kids to become readers, to become comfortable with a book, not **daunted**. Books shouldn't be daunting, they should be funny, exciting and wonderful…"

Dahl once said, "Those who do not believe in magic will never find it." Maybe that is why people love his work so much. His stories are full of magic, and we want to believe in magic. Mr. Dahl died in 1990, but his stories will live forever.

"Roald Dahl"—Think About It

1. What is the purpose of this text?

_____

_____

_____

2. Why did Mr. Dahl think he was good at writing children's stories?

_____

_____

_____

_____

3. What do you think the word _daunted_ means? Why?

_____

_____

_____

_____

4. What did Mr. Dahl think was needed to make children want to read?

_____

_____

_____

_____

"Roald Dahl"—Think About It (continued)

5. Why do you think the author used quotations by Roald Dahl in this text? How is the information the author gives different from the quotations?

_____

_____

_____

_____

_____

6. What was one reason the author gives as to why Mr. Dahl wrote stories for children? Do you think this reason might be true? Why or why not?

_____

_____

_____

_____

_____

_____

7. Do you have a favorite author? If so, who is the author and why do you like their books?

_____

_____

_____

_____

8. What characteristics do you think a good children's author needs to have? Explain your thinking.

_____

_____

_____

Spider-Man

Spider-Man is a very popular **comic book super hero**. The first comic book about Spider-Man came out in 1963. Since then, 700 different Spider-Man comic books have been **published**. **TV shows** have been made about Spider-Man. Some of these were **animated cartoons** and some had live actors. Five movies about Spider-Man have been made so far.

What Are Spider-Man's Powers?

All super heroes have special powers. Spider-Man got his powers when a **radioactive** spider bit him. The bite made him extra strong for his size and very fast. He can jump huge **distances**. He can **cling** to walls. He has the ability to know when danger is close. This is called his **"spidey-sense."** To help him use these powers better, Spider-Man invented **"web-shooters"** that he wears on his wrists. They shoot out material like a web so he can swing between things.

Who Is Spider-Man?

Spider-Man's real name is Peter Parker. In the first comic book, Peter was 15 years old. He was an orphan who lived with an aunt and uncle. Peter was very smart in school in science. But he was very shy. Some of his classmates were very cruel to him. Then he was bitten by the spider.

As Peter grew older, he **graduated** from high school and went to college. He worked as a **photographer** for a newspaper. But his main job was fighting bad people. To do this, he wore a **disguise** so no one would know who he was.

Why Is Spider-Man So Popular?

Spider-Man is popular because he is just like other people. Peter Parker went to school. He got a job to make money. He had problems with friends. Young people can understand him because he is young too. The super powers that make him Spider-Man do not make him different. He is still Peter Parker.

Readers also like Spider-Man because he uses his powers for good. He never gives up. He does not use powerful **weapons** to hurt people. He can do amazing things with his body that help him stop his **enemies**. And he has a really cool **costume**!

"Spider-Man"—Think About It

1. What proof does the author give to show that Spider-Man is a popular super hero?

_____

_____

_____

2. What is the difference between an animated show and one with live actors?

_____

_____

3. What is Spider-Man's "spidey-sense?"

_____

_____

4. Give two reasons why the author thinks Spider-Man is popular.

_____

_____

5. This is a *descriptive text*. What does this mean? Give examples to explain your answer.

_____

_____

_____

6. The headings in this text are questions. How do these questions help you predict what the text will tell you?

_____

_____

_____

Who Was Paul Bunyan?

Paul Bunyan is a famous **folk tale** character. But even **imaginary** characters have to come from somewhere. How did the tales about Paul Bunyan start?

Many people believe that the stories about Paul Bunyan started with **French-Canadian lumberjacks** in Quebec in the 1800s. His original name was Paul Bonjean, or Bonyenne. As the stories were passed from camp to camp, and into English-speaking Canada and the United States, his name was changed to Bunyan.

The first written tale about Paul Bunyan appeared in 1906 in a Detroit, Michigan, newspaper. The author wrote it based on a tale he had heard in a **logging camp**. Many other tales followed, written by different people. Paul Bunyan was even featured in a logging company's **advertisements**. In the 1920s, the stories began changing from tales about the hard life in logging camps to children's stories. Paul Bunyan became even more popular when TV shows and movies were made about him.

Why is Paul Bunyan a folk hero? Maybe it is because he is a **symbol** of **strength** and **hard work**. But I think it is just because the tales are funny. Here are a few "facts" about Paul and his companion, Babe the Blue Ox.

- Paul so was large when he was born that five storks had to carry him to his parents.
- One day Paul was having trouble clearing trees along a **crooked** road. He tied a piece of rope to one end of the road and Babe to the other. Babe pulled with all his **strength** until the road became **straight**.
- Paul created the **Grand Canyon** by dragging a special logging tool on the ground.
- Paul chased all the whales out of the St. Lawrence River by trying to **harness** them to pull logs.
- Paul scooped out the Great Lakes to make **drinking holes** for Babe.
- Paul cut down all the trees in North and South Dakota to make farmland.

"Who Was Paul Bunyan?"—Think About It

1. How did the tales about Paul Bunyan change as they became more popular?

_____

_____

2. What do you think happened to the stories as they were passed from camp to camp? Why?

_____

_____

_____

3. Read this sentence from the text: Here are a few "facts" about Paul and his companion, Babe the Blue Ox. Why does the word _facts_ have quotation marks around it?

_____

_____

4. What is this text about? Write a short summary about its main ideas.

_____

_____

_____

5. The author says that people like Paul Bunyan because the tales are funny. What evidence does the author give to support this idea?

_____

_____

_____

6. List three "facts" that Paul Bunyan and Babe the Blue Ox are said to be responsible for.

_____

_____

_____

Marie Curie

Marie Curie was very **humble** and **shy**. If you had passed her on the street, you would likely never have known that she was one of the most **famous scientists** ever. Marie was not only the first woman to win the **world's top science prize**, she was also the first person to win it twice.

Little Marya

Marie was born in Warsaw, Poland, in 1867. Her Polish name was Marya Skłodowska (say it like this: *MAR-ee-ah Skwa-DOFF-ska*). She was always at the top of her class in school but, at that time, women were not allowed to go to the university in Poland.

When Marie was 23, she left Poland to study science in Paris, France. There, she met Pierre Curie, who liked science as much as she did. Most men give candy and flowers to women they like. Not Pierre. He gave Marie one of his science reports! The couple fell in love, married, and began working together.

Remarkable Radiation

Marie started examining **rocks** that contained the metal **uranium**. She knew another scientist had discovered uranium gives off **invisible rays**, called **radiation**. Marie and Pierre decided to find out more about these rays.

Marie soon discovered new metals that also gave off radiation. She named one **polonium**, after her home country of Poland, and the other **radium**, because it sounds like "radiation." Marie and Pierre's work with radiation earned the couple a **Nobel Prize**—the most important science award in the world.

Brave Marie

Sadly, just three years later, Pierre was in an accident and died. Marie continued her work and won another Nobel Prize in 1911.

World War I broke out in 1914 and France was soon under attack. Marie wanted to do all she could to help French soldiers. She loaded cars with **X-ray equipment** and she and other **volunteers** drove them to the **battlefields**.

The equipment helped doctors diagnose injuries quickly. Marie taught many other women how to use the X-ray machines. By the time the war ended in 1918, she had helped save the lives of many people.

Marie's Legacy

Scientists now know that the radiation Marie discovered has many uses. **Radiation therapy** is used to **treat cancer**. People use radiation to **produce electricity**, and **kill organisms** that spoil food. Radiation is also used in **smoke detectors** and to find **weak** spots in bridges and pipelines.

Perhaps most importantly, Marie's work still **encourages** girls to become scientists.

Fun Facts
- Marie graduated from high school at 15 years old. She was the top student in her class.
- After Pierre died, Marie took over his job as a professor at the Sorbonne University in Paris, France. She was the first woman to teach there.
- Marie became good friends with scientist Albert Einstein.
- Marie earned her first Nobel Prize in physics, and her second Nobel Prize in chemistry.
- The notebooks that Marie used while working with uranium still give off radiation.

"Marie Curie"—Think About It

1. What characteristics would you use to describe Marie? Use details from the text to support your answer.

_____

_____

_____

2. How did Marie help save lives during World War I?

_____

_____

3. Marie won her first Nobel Prize in 1903 and her second in 1911. How old was she each time?

_____

4. What are two details about Marie you learned under the subheading Little Marya?

_____

_____

5. Marie once said, "One never notices what has been done; one can only see what remains to be done." What do you think this says about what kind of person she was?

_____

_____

6. Why do you think Marie's work encourages girls to become scientists?

_____

_____

7. What are some of the different ways that radiation is used?

_____

_____

Annie Oakley

Imagine being able to shoot a rifle and split a playing card edge-on, then put several more holes in the card before it hit the ground. That is what Annie Oakley could do!

Annie Oakley was not her real name. She was born Phoebe Ann Moses on August 13, 1860, in western Ohio. She had a tough childhood because her family was very poor. Instead of going to school, Phoebe had to work hard.

To help her family, Phoebe began shooting and trapping animals when she was just eight years old. She was a good shot right from the beginning. Restaurants, hotels, and neighbors bought the animals she hunted and she was able to help her family. That was always very important to her.

The Wild West

Phoebe married another sharpshooter, Frank Butler, when she was just 16. They began performing together on stage, amazing people with their skill and accuracy. Phoebe began performing under the stage name "Annie Oakley." With a shot from her rifle, Annie could hit a dime that was tossed up into the air. She could snuff out a burning candle with a bullet. Annie could also shoot an object far behind her while she looked over her shoulder with a mirror.

Native American leader Sitting Bull saw Annie perform at the show. He was so impressed with her character and her skill that he wanted to adopt her as his daughter! He gave Annie the name "Little Sure Shot."

In 1885, Annie and Frank joined the famous Buffalo Bill's Wild West show. Audiences loved Annie and her incredible shooting tricks. Annie and Frank toured the United States and Europe with the Wild West show. They performed for many important people, including monarchs and royals such as Queen Victoria of England and Kaiser Wilhelm II of Germany. The Kaiser even asked to be in their show. So Annie had him stand facing the audience, then she shot off the tip of a small item the Kaiser was holding between his lips!

The Western Girl

After performing with the Wild West show for many years, Annie left to perform in the play *The Western Girl*. The show was written especially for her and her incredible talents. In it, she used a pistol, rifle, and rope to escape a group of outlaws.

Annie suffered a number of car and train accidents, but managed to recover each time. When she was more than 60 years old, she still performed her fantastic tricks and set records.

First American Female Superstar

Annie's skills and hard work made her the first female superstar in the United States. But Annie also thought it was important for women to be fit, and to know how to defend themselves from criminals.

Annie taught thousands of women how to use a gun safely. She also worked hard for women's rights.

Fun Facts

- People were often surprised when they first met Annie. They were expecting a big, tough woman, but Annie had a quiet voice and was only 5 feet (1.5 meters) tall.
- Annie shot pennies off her nephew's head when he was a boy. He said he was never scared because his aunt never missed.
- Annie was very shy in person and would not look people in the eye when talking to them. Instead, she stared at the top of their heads or their ears, which reportedly made some people very uncomfortable.
- In 1913, Annie and Frank retired and settled in Cambridge, Maryland. The couple adopted a dog named Dave, who performed in their later shows.
- Annie had been the top earner in the Wild West show and she shared her good fortune with her family. She also gave money to orphan charities.
- During World War I, Annie offered to organize a regiment of female sharpshooters. The army did not accept her offer, so she raised money for the Red Cross instead by performing at army camps.
- During her retirement, Annie did a lot of hunting and fishing. She also taught women how to shoot accurately.
- In the early 1920s, Annie and Frank were both severely injured in a car accident. After she recovered, Annie returned to performing for about a month.
- In 1946, famous composer Irving Berlin wrote a Broadway musical about Annie's life called Annie Get Your Gun. The musical was adapted into a movie in 1950.

"Annie Oakley"—Think About It

1. What characteristics would you use to describe Annie? Use details from the text to support your answer.

_____

_____

_____

2. What does the word *sharpshooter* mean? Use details from the text to support your answer.

_____

3. Who gave Annie the nickname "Little Sure Shot"?

_____

4. How did Annie help people throughout her life? Use details from the text to support your answer.

_____

_____

_____

_____

5. What three things could Annie do with her rifle? Use specific details from the text.

_____

_____

_____

6. How did Annie involve Kaiser Wilhelm II of Germany in one of her shows?

_____

_____

7. What was the name of the famous person who wrote a musical about Annie's life?

_____

The Goose and the Golden Eggs
(Based on a fable by Aesop)

There was once a poor man who lived in a village. Every day, he walked through the village looking for someone who could give him a little work. When he was lucky, he earned enough money to buy one small meal.

One day, the man saw a fat goose run by, so he chased after it and caught it. "What a **hearty** meal you will make!" said the man. "Tonight my stomach will be full for a change."

"Do not eat me!" cried the goose. "I am a goose like no other. If you feed me and take care of me, I will lay golden eggs for you."

"Can this be true?" the man wondered. "Since this **remarkable** goose can talk, perhaps it can lay golden eggs, too. I will give it a chance." So the man took the goose home and fed it the last few **scraps** of food in his cupboard, even though he had to go to bed hungry that night.

As soon as he awoke the next morning, the man rushed over to the goose. Under the goose he found a large, shiny egg made of **solid gold**. He took the egg to the market and sold it for lots of money. When he came home, his arms were full of food, including good food for the goose. The man had lots of money left over in his pocket.

Each day, the goose laid another golden egg and the man sold it, making sure he brought home good food for the goose. Before long, the man was very rich, yet he wanted to become even richer. "Why should I spend so much money on food for the goose?" he asked himself. He decided to cut the goose open. That way, he could get all the golden eggs at once and no longer would he have to spend money on food for the goose.

The man cut open the goose and found no golden eggs. "What have I done?" he cried. "Now the goose is dead and I will have no more golden eggs!"

"The Goose and the Golden Eggs"—Think About It

1. a) Use clues in the fable to help you explain how a hearty meal is different from the meals the man ate before he caught the goose.

_____

_____

b) What two clues in the fable help you understand what *hearty* means?

_____

_____

2. The goose in the fable can talk. Explain why this convinces the man that it might also be true that the goose can lay golden eggs.

_____

_____

_____

3. The man made sure he bought good food for the goose, not just any kind of food. Why did the man want to buy good food for the goose?

_____

_____

_____

4. Choose the lesson, or moral, that best fits the fable. Then explain why you think the moral fits the fable.
   ☐ If you are greedy, you may lose what you have instead of gaining more.
   ☐ Never trust a goose that can talk.
   ☐ Always be sure to feed a goose good food.

_____

_____

_____

_____

The Rich Miser (Based on a fable by Aesop)

There was once a man named Nicholas who was the **richest** person in town. But Nicholas was a **miser**, so he hated spending money. He bought no nice clothes, bought no one gifts, and gave no money to the poor.

Everyone in the town knew that Nicholas was a wealthy miser. When he walked in the street, children danced around him calling, "Miser! Miser!" Nicholas did not mind. He thought only about his **pile of money** and how happy it made him. Soon he began to fear that someone would steal it.

"I will take all my money and buy a huge lump of gold," thought Nicholas. "Then I will bury it where no one will find it." That is just what he did. He buried the gold in a hole outside the town. Every night, he crept out to the hole and dug up his gold to make sure it was still there. Nothing made him as happy as **gazing** at the huge lump of gold.

Soon, the townspeople **noticed** that Nicholas was **sneaking** out of his house every night. People grew **curious** and, before long, someone discovered the gold and ran away with the **treasure**.

The next night, Nicholas saw that his treasure was gone. "Someone has stolen my lump of gold!" he cried over and over, howling with **grief**. Soon the noise drew a crowd of townspeople.

"Do you want your **precious** gold back?" asked one old woman. "Just drop a heavy stone in the hole and pretend it is your gold."

"How can you **mock** me at a time like this?" asked Nicholas.

"I'm not making fun of you," said the old woman. "All you did with your precious treasure was **gaze** at it every night. You could do the very same thing with a stone."

Nicholas was speechless. He hung his head in **shame** and went home.

"The Rich Miser"—Think About It

1. Use clues from the fable to complete the definitions below.

a) A miser is someone who _____

b) Someone who is wealthy has _____

c) When you mock someone, you are _____

2. How do you think someone discovered where Nicholas had hidden his gold?

_____

_____

_____

3. At the end of the fable, Nicholas has nothing to say. Why did he not argue with the old woman?

_____

_____

_____

4. Choose the lesson, or moral, that best fits this story. Then explain why you think the moral fits the story.

☐ Do not try to sneak out of your house at night.

☐ There is no point in having lots of money if you do not spend it.

☐ Never let people call you a miser.

_____

_____

_____

_____

_____

The Rich Man and the Thief
(Based on an African folktale)

There was once a thief who **sneaked** into a rich man's house and **stole** a bag of gold. "I bet that rich man has even more gold **hidden** somewhere," said the thief. "I will go back tomorrow and try to find it."

The next day, the thief went back to the rich man's house when he thought the man would be out. He was just about to sneak in the back door when the rich man opened a window. "Can I help you?" asked the rich man. The thief was **startled** and could not think of what to say, so he just ran away.

"What a **strange** way to act," thought the rich man. "I bet that is the thief who stole from me yesterday. I will tell the **judge** about this."

The judge listened to the rich man's story. "Find this man and bring him to me," said the judge. "Then I will find out if he stole your money."

When the thief heard that the judge wanted to see him, he knew he might be in big **trouble**. He went to an old woman who was supposed to be very **wise** and asked for her **advice**. "I will give you half the money I stole if you will help me," promised the thief. The old woman **agreed** to help.

"Go home and dress in rags," said the old woman. "Rub dirt all over your face. Then go to see the judge. When he asks you a question, rub your head and say 'Moo!' Then you will not get in any trouble."

The thief did exactly what the old woman had said. Every time the judge asked him a question, he rubbed his head and said, 'Moo!'

"This man must be crazy," said the judge. "I have no way to tell if he is guilty. Let him go." The thief was **overjoyed**.

The next day, the old woman went to the thief and asked for the money he had promised her. The thief just rubbed his head and said, "Moo!" The old woman gave up and went home without her money.

MOO!

98

"The Rich Man and the Thief"—Think About It

1. a) What does *startled* mean in this story?

_____

b) Use details from the story to explain why your definition of *startled* makes sense.

_____

_____

2. Give two events in the story that show the thief is very greedy.

_____

_____

_____

3. Why did the rich man suspect that the thief was the person who had stolen his money?

_____

_____

4. Give evidence from the story to show that the old woman is both wise and foolish.

Evidence that the old woman is wise:

_____

_____

Evidence that the old woman is foolish:

_____

_____

5. What lesson or moral does this story teach?

_____

_____

Graphic Organizers

Graphic organizers are excellent tools to use for identifying and organizing information from a text into an easy-to-understand visual format. Students will expand their comprehension of a text as they complete the graphic organizers. Use these graphic organizers in addition to the activities in this book or with other texts.

Concept Web – Helps students understand the main idea of a text and how it is supported by key details.

Concept Map – Helps students gain a better understanding of how different subtopics within a text connect to the topic as a whole.

Venn Diagram/Comparison Chart – Helps students focus on the comparison of two items, such as individuals, ideas, events, or pieces of information. Students could compare by looking at which things are the same, or contrast by looking at which things are different.

Fact or Opinion – Helps students to distinguish between statements of fact or opinion. Facts are pieces of information that can be proven to be true. Opinions are pieces of information based on something that someone thinks or believes, but that cannot necessarily be proven to be true.

Cause and Effect – Helps students to recognize and explain relationships between events. The cause is the reason why an event happens and the effect is the event that happens.

Making Connections – Helps students to connect something they have read, or experienced, with the world around them.

Context Clue Chart – Helps students organize clues that the author gives in a text to help define a difficult or unusual word. Encourage students to look for explanations of words within a text.

Drawing Conclusions and Making Inferences Chart – Helps students practice drawing conclusions and making inferences based on their prior knowledge, as well as what they read in the text.

A Concept Web About...

A **main idea** is what the text is mostly about. A **detail** is important information that tells more about the main idea.

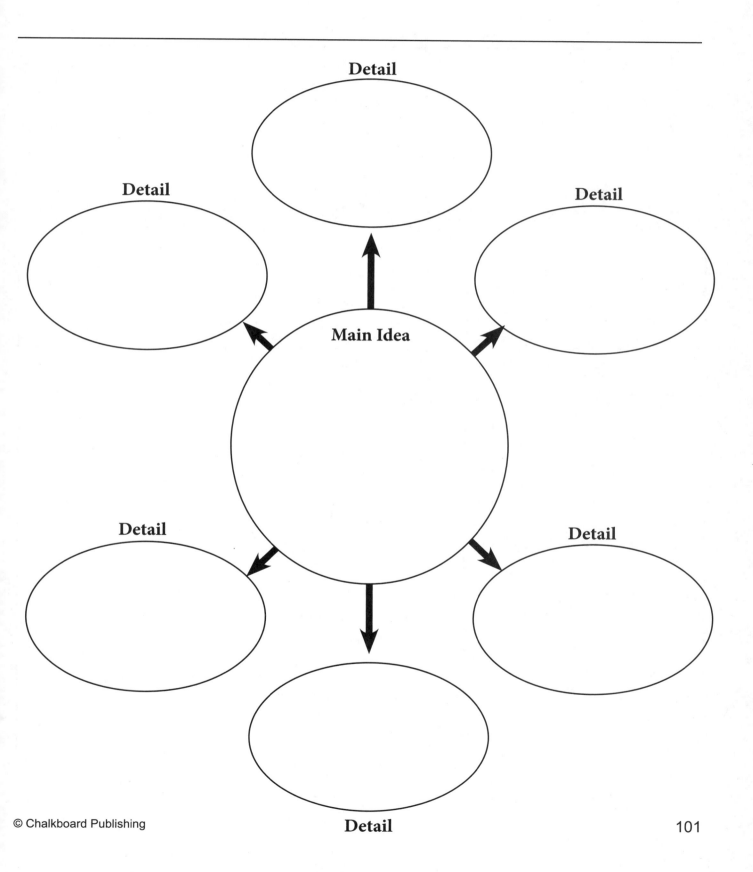

Detail

Detail

Detail

Main Idea

Detail

Detail

Detail

Concept Map

A **main idea** is what the text is mostly about.
A **subheading** is the title given to a part of a text.
A **detail** is important information that tells more about the main idea.

Main Idea

Subheading

Subheading

Subheading

Details

Details

Details

A Venn Diagram About...

_____

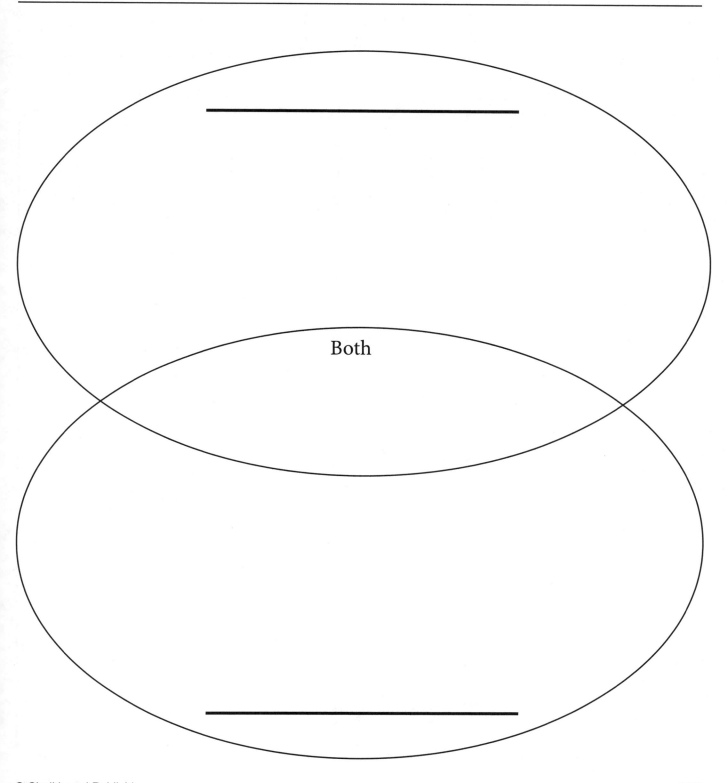

Both

A Comparison Chart

Compared to

Detailed information

Detailed information

Fact or Opinion

- **Facts** are pieces of information that can be proven to be true.
- **Opinions** are pieces of information based on something a person thinks or believes.

Piece of Information	Fact or Opinion?	How do you know?

Cause and Effect

- The **cause** is the reason something happens.
- The **effect** is what happened.

Cause   **Effect**

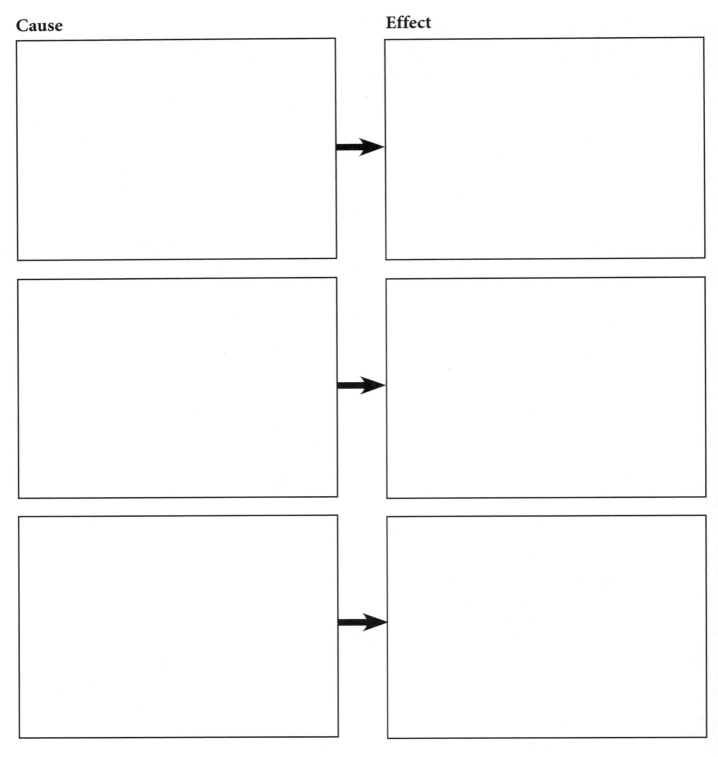

Making Connections with What I Have Read

After reading…	It reminds me of…	This helps me make a connection to…
		☐ something else I have read ☐ myself ☐ the world around me
		☐ something else I have read ☐ myself ☐ the world around me
		☐ something else I have read ☐ myself ☐ the world around me
		☐ something else I have read ☐ myself ☐ the world around me

Context Clue Chart

Context Clues are hints that the author gives in a text that can help you find the meaning of a word.

Word	Context Clue from Text	Meaning of Word

Drawing Conclusions and Making Inferences Chart

We make an **inference** when we combine what we know to be true with new information and come to a conclusion.

What I already know:

Clues from the text I read:

Help me to conclude or infer:

How Am I Doing?

	Completing my work	Using my time wisely	Following directions	Keeping organized
Full speed ahead!	• My work is always complete and done with care. • I added extra details to my work.	• I always get my work done on time.	• I always follow directions.	• My materials are always neatly organized. • I am always prepared and ready to learn.
Keep going!	• My work is complete and done with care. • I added extra details to my work.	• I usually get my work done on time.	• I usually follow directions without reminders.	• I usually can find my materials. • I am usually prepared and ready to learn.
Slow down!	• My work is complete. • I need to check my work.	• I sometimes get my work done on time.	• I sometimes need reminders to follow directions.	• I sometimes need time to find my materials. • I am sometimes prepared and ready to learn.
Stop!	• My work is not complete. • I need to check my work.	• I rarely get my work done on time.	• I need reminders to follow directions.	• I need to organize my materials. • I am rarely prepared and ready to learn.

Reading Comprehension Student Tracking Sheet

Student's Name	Identifies the Purpose of the Text *Student: I can tell you why we read this.*	Demonstrates Understanding of the Text *Student: I can tell you what the text is about.*	Analyzes Text *Student: I can make predictions, interpretations, and conclusions using information from the text.*	Makes Connections to Text (Prior Knowledge) *Student: This reminds me of* • *tex-to-text* • *text-to-self* • *text-to-world*	Text Features *Student: I can tell you how different text features help the reader.*

Level 4: Student shows a thorough understanding of all or almost all concepts and consistently gives appropriate and complete explanations independently. No teacher support is needed.

Level 3: Student shows a good understanding of most concepts and usually gives complete or nearly complete explanations. Infrequent teacher support is needed.

Level 2: Student shows a satisfactory understanding of most concepts and sometimes gives appropriate, but incomplete explanations. Teacher support is sometimes needed.

Level 1: Student shows little understanding of concepts and rarely gives complete explanations. Intensive teacher support is needed.

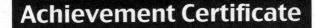

You Are Doing Incredible!

Keep Up the Good Work!

_____
Name

_____
Date